THE SOCIAL
ENTREPRENEUR

THE SOCIAL ENTREPRENEUR

The Business of
Changing the World

edited by
Robert A. Danielson

Paperback ISBN: 978-1-62824-237-9
Mobi ISBN: 978-1-62824-238-6
ePub ISBN: 978-1-62824-239-3
uPDF ISBN: 978-1-62824-340-9

Library of Congress Control Number: 2015954071

Cover design by Nikabrik Design
Page design by PerfecType

Published in conjunction with
The Office of Faith, Work, and Economics
Asbury Theological Seminary
Wilmore, Kentucky

SEEDBED PUBLISHING
Franklin, Tennessee
Seedbed.com
Sow for a Great Awakening

CONTENTS

CHAPTER ONE

WHAT IS SOCIAL ENTREPRENEURSHIP?

David Bosch

A Picture of Social Entrepreneurship

The Loft Coffee Shop just outside of San Antonio serves fresh pastries, a full lunch, a waffle bar on Saturday mornings, and coffee and specialty drinks. Most people are unaware at first that this enterprise is actually a work of Riverside, a United Methodist church. In fact, Riverside was birthed out of The Loft Coffee Shop. The Loft Coffee Shop's stated goal is to "provide . . . a quiet respite . . . a place for community gatherings and activities . . . to give back locally and internationally . . . to breathe life into others" (Gosnell 2010). The Loft wanted to engage the culture and create community instead of following the older church model of erecting a church building and assuming people would come. The Loft has drawn people who would not normally be drawn to a church. They have also provided a space for Bible studies, mom's groups, and teenage groups. They not only began a church, but they formed the Hope Center—a combination thrift store, food pantry, and social service resource referral service.

The Loft Coffee Shop is a picture of social entrepreneurship. In the coming pages we are going to explore even further what social entrepreneurship is and who is the social entrepreneur. Additionally, we will discover the importance of being intentional about the multifaceted nature of social entrepreneurship. Finally, we will explore some initial next steps for involvement.

What Is Social Entrepreneurship?

To answer this question, we first have to answer the question: What is entrepreneurship? Entrepreneurship is the activity related to taking initiative to innovate and create. Thus, entrepreneurs are instrumental in the creation of new enterprises, the growth of the economy, the promotion of learning, and innovation in the world. This is true of both the commercial entrepreneur that is engaged primarily in growing the economy, but also for social entrepreneurs that are motivated by fostering positive social change. Because of this, government leaders, business incubators, development organizations, and academic institutions are interested in encouraging entrepreneurial activity. Christians and their churches also need to be involved in encouraging this entrepreneurial activity.

Social entrepreneurship, which involves starting an organization with the resolve of achieving positive social change, has been on the rise in recent decades. The study of social entrepreneurship has also been increasing in recent years, but there are no clear definitions of what it is exactly. Some researchers have found it to only apply to nonprofit ventures (Thompson 2002), while others see it as a hybrid model of sorts where profits are generated in order to fulfill the organization's social mission (Nicholls 2010).

While there are many definitions of social entrepreneurship, most see it as referring to the creation of organizations attempting to impact positive social change. Professor J. Gregory Dees (1988) contended that social entrepreneurs develop organizations along a continuum of enterprises ranging from purely philanthropic to purely commercial (see Table One). However, Dees (2001) stated the distinguishing feature of social entrepreneurship is keeping the social mission central and explicit. Thus, Dees described social entrepreneurs as being focused on social value creation by advancing a positive social change. Dees's definition is the most commonly used and cited in the social entrepreneurship literature.

The Social Enterprise Spectrum (Adapted from Dees)			
	Purely Philanthropic	◄──────►	Purely Commercial
Motives, Methods, Goals	Appeal to Goodwill; Mission-Driven Social Value	Mixed Motives; Mission- & Market-Driven Social & Economic Value	Appeal to Self-Interest; Market-Driven Economic Value
Beneficiaries	Pay Nothing	Subsidized Rates, or Mix of Full Payers and Those Who Pay Nothing	Market-Rate Prices
Capital	Donations & Grants	Below-Market Capital, or Mix of Donations and Market-Capital	Market-Rate Capital
Workforce	Volunteers	Below-Market Wages, or Mix of Volunteers and Fully Paid Staff	Market-Rate Compensation
Suppliers	In-Kind Donations	Special Discount, or Mix of In-Kind and Full-Price Donations	Market-Rate Prices

Table One

As mentioned, one of the key attributes of social entrepreneurship is the focus on social value creation. It is true that purely commercial entrepreneurship has a social aspect, as individuals are engaged in exchange and social value is created through the process of conducting business. However, what makes social entrepreneurship distinctive from purely commercial entrepreneurship is the primary focus on social value creation rather than economic value. As we will see, this is most likely driven by altruistic reasons and a concern for others. Thus, the driving motivation of social entrepreneurs is social value for the public good.

Isn't This Just Business as Mission?

Some may argue that from a Christian perspective social entrepreneurship is the same thing as "Business as Mission" or BAM. BAM is a term used to describe many different aspects of Christians involved in business. According to authors Neal Johnson and Steven Rundle (2006), many people use the terms "Tentmaking," "Marketplace Ministry," and "Business as Mission" synonymously, causing confusion in the discussion. However, all of these terms can also have distinct meanings; therefore, it is important to clarify the differences between social entrepreneurship and Business as Mission. Thus, in regards to this discussion, the term "Business as Mission" is defined in a way that is consistent with the first think tank held on BAM in Thailand, which laid out four distinctives (Tunehag, McGee, and Plummer 2004):

+ BAM is profitable and sustainable
+ Intentional about kingdom of God purposes and impact on people and nations
+ Focused on transformation and multiple bottom lines
+ Focused on the world's poorest and least evangelized

Even more specifically, Rundle (2014) reports that there appears to be a consensus around key elements—such as BAM is self-funded, laity-driven, intentional, holistic, and cross-cultural. Because of this distinction, BAM is not the Christian business person that works for a company (local or multinational) in a cross-cultural context, nor is it businesses that happen to be run by Christians (unless they are being intentional about transformation and focused on the world's poorest and least evangelized). Finally, this definition also excludes businesses that Christians establish as a cover, front, or means to have access to people. What distinguishes BAM from social entrepreneurship is BAM's focus on the world's poorest and least evangelized in a cross-cultural context. Social entrepreneurship operates in a broader context. Therefore, in many ways, BAM can be viewed as a subset of social entrepreneurship, but not synonymous with social entrepreneurship.

Who Is the Social Entrepreneur?

Becoming an entrepreneur, starting an organization, is a planned behavior and an intentional act (Bird 1988). Hence, the essence of entrepreneurship—the creation of new enterprises—is essentially the same regardless of whether it is for profit or for social reasons (Mair and Noboa 2003). There are common characteristics of those who intend to start an organization, some of which are the following:

* Creativity
* Innovation
* A family history of entrepreneurship
* An ability to recognize opportunity and to take advantage of it

As stated above, the mission of social entrepreneurs is social value for the public good. Thus, even though the essence of entrepreneurship is similar for both the commercial and social entrepreneur, the motivations between the two are different (Mair and Noba 2003). Since values impact motivations and behaviors, there appear to be differences in personal values for individuals with social entrepreneurial intent. Therefore, an understanding of values is necessary in order to understand how values could impact a person's intention to start a social venture.

Values may be related to an individual's self-identity, and as such they influence and regulate an individual's behaviors (Lord and Brown 2001) as they serve as guiding principles around which one bases life decisions. Furthermore, individuals find meaning in work by doing work that is in congruence with their value system (Ros, Schwartz, and Surkiss 2007). Therefore, it would make sense that social entrepreneurs would be altruistic and others-centered, since social entrepreneurship involves impacting change so that people's lives are transformed in a positive way. In fact, in a recent study, openness to change and benevolence were positively related to social entrepreneurial intent (Bosch 2013). Other research (Mair and Noboa 2003) has found that social entrepreneurs have the following values:

- Others-directed
- Empathy
- Benevolence
- Charity
- Consideration for others

The Importance of Intentionality

Because a major distinctive of social entrepreneurship is the desire for social value creation, the social entrepreneur has to be intentional in determining the impact of the social venture. There has been a push to measure this impact much like commercial entrepreneurs value wealth creation by measuring profit. As a result, social entrepreneurs measure not just the economic bottom line of profit but also multiple bottom lines. Much like the multiple definitional differences in social entrepreneurship, there are multiple variations of the bottom lines that social entrepreneurs should measure. Most all agree, however, that the economic bottom line of profit should be measured— even in non-profit entities. Likewise, there is wide agreement that social capital should be measured. Environmental impact is often discussed as the third bottom line to measure, while Christian ventures tend to measure spiritual impact as the third bottom line. The main thing to be aware of is that, depending upon who is discussing the issue, they may define triple and multiple bottom lines differently. We have decided to describe multiple bottom lines as the "triple bottom line," made up of the following categories:

1. Economic
2. Social
3. Spiritual

Economic Capital

Economic capital is economic sustainability. For those social enterprises operating on the left side of Dees's (1988) spectrum of being purely philanthropic, this is an issue of being good stewards of the donors' gifts and contributions. This can be measured in terms of fee growth, donation growth for future and expanded work, working capital, and even net profitability.

For social enterprises operating on the right side of the continuum of being purely commercial, profitability is one of the most important factors in terms of economic sustainability. Author Ken Eldred (2005) calls profit the lifeblood of a company. If a social enterprise is not relying on outside donors or financial assistance, it is not sustainable or able to produce social and spiritual capital if it is not profitable. Without profits a company is unable to grow, employ and serve more people, or protect itself against economic fluctuations and downturns. This can be measured by revenue growth, net income, working capital, and other profitability metrics such as return on assets (ROA) and return on investment (ROI).

Social Capital

Social capital relates to the justice and relational themes found in Scripture. Social capital is in line with John Wesley's view of service for the public good, that a love of neighbor flows from a love of God. Beyond just being concerned for the shareholders of an organization, growing social capital relates to being concerned for the stakeholders of the organization. Thus, the organization needs to be cognizant of the employees, suppliers, customers, program recipients, and communities in which the organization works. Social capital is relationship-based and it is relationship-driven.

Since the distinguishing feature of social entrepreneurship is creating positive social change, this is a key area of emphasis in social ventures. Some social ills that social enterprises focus on are environmental concerns, poverty, literacy, unemployment, human trafficking, and job skill development, to name a few. Therefore, the social ill that an enterprise is focused on will determine what and how they will measure their social capital.

Spiritual Capital

Spiritual capital is the most important element of the triple bottom line as it sets the tone for how economic and social capital is created. Because of the importance of spiritual capital, the social enterprise needs to be explicit about the outcomes they hope to obtain, as well as how they will measure the impact. This is also one of the most difficult areas to measure impact, as one cannot adequately know an individual's spiritual growth.

Because spiritual capital is the most important element of the three, faith must be integrated throughout the enterprise. Dishonest business practices or exploitive labor practices, as two of many examples, may lead to short-term growth in economic capital, but harm will be done to both social and spiritual capital. Because faith integration throughout the operation of the organization is so important, author Neal Johnson (2009) recommends developing a master plan so that the organization can be intentional about its faith integration.

The Loft Coffee Shop is one picture of social entrepreneurship practicing a triple bottom line. A new enterprise was created that has at its core a vision to create social change and add social value. The revenues (economic capital) from the coffee shop, thrift center, and food pantry are used to sustain the organization. The coffee shop and the thrift center have created community and provided services and help to those in need, which is an example of social capital. Finally, spiritual capital in the forms of Bible studies, changed lives, and the birth of a church has occurred as a result of this social venture.

How Can I Get Involved?

Now that we know what social entrepreneurship is and that values motivate social entrepreneurs, what are the next steps? One way is by bringing one's dormant values, values that the individual already possesses, to the surface. Through the influence of a transformational leader, individuals can learn values over time and through socialization. So, practically, one should be mentored by leaders who are others-directed, benevolent, charitable, and empathetic. Additionally, as a part of the socialization process, an individual should attend workshops and conferences to learn more about what social ventures are doing and how social entrepreneurs started in order to stimulate their dormant values and increase their self-efficacy for starting a social venture.

Finally, for organizational leaders and others of influence, like pastors and church leaders, it is imperative to understand the spectrum of organizations that can be involved in social entrepreneurship. Since the values related to social justice and benevolence are more strongly associated with individuals with social entrepreneurial intent, and power, achievement, creativity, stimulation, and independence are more highly associated with individuals with commercial entrepreneurial intent, it may be helpful for organizational leaders to understand the specific values of the individual they are working with to guide them in entrepreneurial activities that are congruent with their value system. For example, an individual that places a high value on achievement and independence may be unaware of the broad avenues available as a social entrepreneur. An individual may make the faulty assumption that social entrepreneurship is only about nonprofit work, and they may find nonprofit work undesirable. However, social entrepreneurs can launch an organization along a continuum of enterprises from philanthropic to for-profit with the distinguishing feature of focusing on social value creation. Therefore, if an organizational leader is attuned to the individual's personal value system they can help guide them toward an organizational model congruent with their values.

Even more important than understanding an individual's values is understanding the theological underpinnings of social entrepreneurship to help the individual discover how their faith and theology fit into their calling. These areas will be explored in chapters 2 and 3. Finally, from a practical standpoint, the final three chapters will explore getting a local community involved in social entrepreneurship, writing a business plan, and discovering resources to move the plan forward.

Discussion Questions

1. How would you define *social entrepreneurship*? Can you think of examples that come to mind (both international and domestic)?
2. If you were to start a social enterprise, where would it fall on Dees's spectrum from "purely philanthropic" to "purely commercial"? Why?
3. Which of the common characteristics of entrepreneurs do you have? What about of the common values of a social entrepreneur?
4. Do you agree that spiritual capital is the most important of the triple bottom line? Why or why not?
5. Where would you go to find a mentor or transformational leader to learn more about the values of social entrepreneurs?

Works Cited

Bird, Barbara. 1988. "Implementing Entrepreneurial Ideas: The Case for Intention." *Academy of Management Review* 13 (3): 442–53.

Bosch, David A. 2013. *A Comparison of Commercial and Social Entrepreneurial Intent: The Impact of Personal Values.* Doctoral dissertation. Virginia Beach, VA: Regent University.

Dees, J. Gregory. 1988. "Enterprising Non-Profits." *Harvard Business Review* (January–February): 55–67.

———. 2001. "The Meaning of 'Social Entrepreneurship'." Center for the Advancement of Social Entrepreneurship. Durham: Duke University. http://www.entrepreneurship.duke.edu/news-item /the-meaning-of-social-entrepreneurship/.

Eldred, Ken. 2005. *God Is at Work: Transforming People and Nations Through Business.* Ventura: Regal Books.

Gosnell, Lynn. 2010. "The Coffeehouse Church." *Faith and Leadership,* March 1. http://www.faithandleadership.com/features/articles /the-coffeehouse-church?page=full.

Johnson, C. Neal. 2009. *Business as Mission: A Comprehensive Guide to Theory and Practice.* Downers Grove: Intervarsity Press.

Johnson, C. Neal, and Steven L. Rundle. 2006. "Business as Mission: The Distinctives and Challenges of a New Approach to World Mission." In *Business as Mission: From Impoverished to Empowered,* edited by Mike Barnett. Pasadena, CA: William Carey Library.

Lord, Robert G., and Douglas J. Brown. 2001. "Leadership, Values, and Subordinate Self-Concepts." *The Leadership Quarterly* 12 (2): 133–52.

Mair, Johanna, and Ernesto Noboa. 2003. *Social Entrepreneurship: How Intentions to Create a Social Enterprise Get Formed.* Working Paper no. 521. Barcelona, Spain: IESE Business School, Universidad de Navarra.

Nicholls, Alex. 2010. "The Legitimacy of Social Entrepreneurship: Reflexive Isomorphism in a Pre-Paradigmatic Field." *Entrepreneurship Theory and Practice* 34 (4): 611–33.

Ros, Maria, Shalom H. Schwartz, and Soshana Surkiss. 2007. "Basic Individual Values, Work Values, and the Meaning of Work." *Applied Psychology* 48 (1): 49–71.

———. 2014. "Does Donor Support Help or Hinder Business as Mission Practitioners? An Empirical Assessment." *International Bulletin of Missionary Research* 38 (1): 21–26.

Thompson, John L. 2002. "The World of the Social Entrepreneur." *International Journal of Public Sector Management* 15 (5): 412–31.

Tunehag, Mats, Wayne McGee, and Josie Plummer, eds. 2004. *Business as Mission*. Lausanne Occasional Paper no. 59. Produced in Pattaya, Thailand, September 29 to October 5, 2004: Lausanne Committee for World Evangelization.

CHAPTER TWO

THE THEOLOGICAL IMPETUS FOR SOCIAL ENTREPRENEURSHIP

Kevin Brown and Kevin Kinghorn

hapter 1 discussed the meaning of social entrepreneurship, which is an entrepreneurial venture that aims to achieve or enact some designated positive social change through a business enterprise. In contrast to many start-up companies, that identify an opportunity in the market and seek to capitalize on it in order to attain profits, participation in entrepreneurial activity and the open markets that facilitate them can be understood in a deeper, more theological way. The purpose of this chapter is to connect a theology of the person, work, and interdependent love with economic concepts of exchange, production, and specialization.

Created to Work

The first thing we learn about God in the Bible is that God is at work. The opening passages of Genesis reveal the astonishing creativity of God, producing the vast array of intricate life and beauty we find in our world. God proclaims this work "good";

yet, we also find the first hints that God intends for more work to be done. In the Genesis chapter 2 story of God's unfolding creation, we find the intriguing statement that "there was no one to work the ground" (v. 5). God's solution was to create man and give him dominion over the living things and land that God had created, "to work it and take care of it" (v. 15) (Nelson 2011, 24–26).

The creation story in Genesis chapter 1 had already established the distinctive capacity of humans for work in God's world. Uniquely among God's creation, we humans are created in God's own image (v. 27). A measure of God's creative capacity is, amazingly, given to us: the capacity to remember, to analyze, and to imagine new possibilities for the beautiful and the good. God's first instruction to us is to unleash this creative power—"Be fruitful and multiply" (v. 28 NKJV). Far from a coercive command, this wonderfully general instruction serves as an invitation to new possibilities. God has created a huge diversity of materials and living things, endless possibilities for us to interact with the objects around us, and to use our creativity in further shaping our world. And now we are invited to be co-creators with God. We are invited to use our complementary forms, male and female, to create new life. And we are invited to use our creative capacity as God's image-bearers in the world to continue to shape this world. We, of course, are not equal creators with God. Nevertheless, God invites us to join him in his ongoing, creative work, growing in our relationships with him and with one another as we do so (Crouch 2013).

Joining Christ in His Work of Bringing Life

The fuller theological context of our work unfolds with the coming of Jesus Christ and the gift of the Holy Spirit. Jesus' work, we read, is unceasing. He is the one who is always interceding on our behalf (Heb. 7:25) and always engaged in the work of reconciling the world to God (John 5:17; 2 Cor. 5:19). Jesus' work (including his prayers and his sacrificial death) is something he offers up to the Father. As followers of Jesus, our role is to add our work to the work that Christ is already doing. We offer our work to the Father, through the Son, and by the power of the Holy Spirit. This is the full, Christian articulation of the context of human work. Positive godly work is always prompted by the Holy Spirit, and this prompting is always to join Christ in the work he has already started, which again we offer up with Christ to the Father.

So what kind of work are we supposed to be joining Christ in doing? And what are our relationships with one another supposed to look like as we work? These are two distinct questions, although they have a single answer. The kind of work we are supposed to do is summed up succinctly in the Great Commandment: to love God with everything we are and have, and to love others as ourselves (Matt. 22:37–40). Jesus' command was to love as he himself loves (John 15:12). We are invited to join Christ in acts of love, aimed at giving life to others. After all, in describing the work for which he came, Jesus said in John 10:10 that he had come so that others "may have *life*, and have it to the full" (emphasis added). His ministry on earth consisted of a holistic concern for people. While addressing their spiritual condition, he also healed the sick (Matt. 15:30–31), fed the hungry (Matt. 15:32–38), and directed his followers to continue this ministry to those who have varieties of needs (Matt. 25:31–46).

In Christ, the kingdom of God has come to earth; and Christ has begun his work of transforming this earth so that it reflects the abundant life that characterizes heaven. While life has many facets, our highest flourishing as human beings is found only in perfected relationships with God and with others in whom God's Spirit dwells. While our work on earth may involve bringing various aspects of life to others, our ultimate goal will always be to move others toward perfected relationships made possible through Christ.

The Life of Interdependent Love

And now we can see how, in answering the question of what our work *is*, we also answer the question of what God intends our relationships with one another to look like, as we join him in his work in our world. As we work together as Christ's body, our relationships with one another are to mirror the eternal relationships of the Triune God. That is, our relationships are to mirror the perfected relationships that exist among Father, Son, and Holy Spirit.

And what is the hallmark of these perfected relationships within the Godhead? Christian orthodox teaching is that the three persons of the Trinity exist eternally and inseparably. While they depend on nothing outside of themselves, they do depend on one another so that they all exist together in relationship, or not at all. Their relationships are ones of love: a pouring out of oneself for the other. The life within God can thus be summarized as a life of interdependent *love*. For humans created in the image of this Trinitarian, relational God, our relationships with one another are perfected inasmuch as they reflect the loving, interdependent relationships among Father, Son, and Holy Spirit (Gutenson 2011, chapters 3 and 4).

The Christian church has always (and rightly) stressed the need for our relationships with one another to be marked by love. Not as much attention has always been placed on the need for our relationships to be marked by interdependence. Jesus' recorded work on earth—as well as God's concern throughout the Old Testament—emphasized outreach to the poor and marginalized. We are right to focus, as God does, on the needs of the voiceless and powerless. And this is not merely because of their material needs. It is also because they are the ones most vulnerable to exclusion from the community of loving, interdependent relationships in which our ultimate flourishing as humans is found.

To be in interdependent relationships is both to receive from others and to give to others. To bring life to the poor and marginalized, we as a Christian, loving community must not merely give to them. We must work to ensure that they are able to give to others in the community as well. Again, the model for our relationships is one of loving interdependence, where everyone is able to pour himself or herself out in love, working to help meet the needs of others.

Wesley on Our Call to Holy Love

John Wesley clearly articulated the connection between our personal growth in Christ and our participation in relationships of loving interdependence. He stated, "The Gospel of Christ knows of no religion, but social; no holiness but social holiness" (Wesley and Wesley 1739, vol. 14, 321). Wesley affirmed that our growth toward the likeness of Christ occurs as we make Jesus Lord of our lives, obeying him with more and more consistency. This obedience is, as we have seen, a matter of joining Christ in his ongoing work of bringing life to others. Thus, for Wesley our personal holiness is tied to the shape of our relationships with others. Holiness is always *social* holiness.

Wesley's theology is perhaps best known for its emphasis on sanctification and growth toward Christian perfection. While Wesley's doctrine of Christian perfection is nuanced and sometimes misunderstood, his summation of our end goal as Christians was simple: "holy love" (Wynkoop 1972). We grow personally in the Lord as our relationships become more and more characterized by holy love. The Father, Son, and Holy Spirit have modeled this holy love for eternity within their own relationships of, once again, loving interdependence.

The call to holy love is a good summation of the theological points outlined so far in this chapter. Our call as Christians is to join our Lord Jesus Christ in bringing abundant life to others. Because others are created in the image of a relational God, abundant life for them will only be possible as they participate in a community of relationships marked by loving interdependence. Our calling is to unleash the creative power God has given us, continuing Christ's work in moving people toward this abundant life.

As we look for others to serve, we must pay special attention to those on the margins—that is, to those most in need of help if they are to be restored to a community of loving interdependence in which they both receive from others and contribute meaningfully to others. Only when communities are marked by this kind of loving interdependence can we truly receive what God wants to give us. A Christian understanding of the common good is that we, as Christ's body, must seek the good things of God together; and we must receive the good things from God together, in community, in relationships with one another. There is no growth in the Lord except social growth in the Lord.

So now the questions before us become: What activities and projects will do this? What works of holy love can we do that will meet others' needs most effectively, and at the same time open up opportunities for them to participate meaningfully, interdependently, within a community of relationships? God has given us, as his image-bearers, a measure of his own creative power. He invites us, indeed commands us and implores us, to use it toward this end.

The Economics of Exchange

To summarize thus far, as image-bearers of God, understanding who God is provides direction as it relates to understanding our own nature. As suggested, part of that nature is bound up in creative work and relational commitments. With this anthropological makeup in mind, we can begin to explore how these key theological insights relate to the idea and practice of social entrepreneurship.

To capture how entrepreneurial activity has the capacity to cultivate the practice of interdependent love, it is important to understand the nature of exchange relationships and trade. If there is one mantra sure to get widespread agreement from all economists, it is this: *trade is good*. But before we get into why, it is helpful to understand the key economic principles behind this mantra.

First, economists believe that people are rational. This term can mean a lot of different things, but here I simply define it as a person who is "goal-seeking." That is, a person who acts on purpose. Second, we live in a world of scarcity. *Scarcity*, defined and described on the first page of nearly every economics textbook, is the problem of having infinite desires in a world of finite resources. Or, in more general terms, scarcity could be summarized by simply acknowledging that there isn't enough to go around. Third, and finally, if rational people find themselves in a world of scarcity, then they will prioritize their decisions. Because resources are limited, and people act rationally, decisions will reflect the course of action that is best, or produces the most benefit (what economists call *utility*) given one's resources.

Trade and Utility

These key economic premises have implications for our cooperative interactions and the mutual benefits inherent in those interactions. Consider an example. Imagine a group of people collected together and provided with a random snack, one per person. The snacks might range from healthy (fruit or whole-grain chips) to unhealthy (candy bars or a twelve-ounce soda). On a scale of one to ten, each person is asked to rate their level of satisfaction with the snack they received (understood as utility or *utils*). Further, accompanied by the rationale as to why they chose this rating, their snack satisfaction score can be recorded. For example, some might say, "I gave my snack a four because raisins give me a headache," or, "I gave this sugar packet a seven because I can put it in my coffee."

Scores would be summed, giving us a total utility score for the group. As one might imagine, randomly distributing the various snacks to various people without considering which snack they actually desire creates an inefficient, or suboptimal, arrangement. The question then arises: What can be done to increase this score? The answer? Trade.

Given this, now imagine creating a second round of snack distribution. This time, each person is allowed to trade with one another over a specified period of time (say, a couple of minutes). Individuals can keep their snack, or opt to exchange. After the trades have occurred, we would have a new utility score, higher (and likely much higher) than the original.

This is a very simple thought exercise, but it demonstrates an important principle in economics: trade allows for mutually beneficial exchange. A rational person would not enter in an exchange with someone else if they did not benefit from that exchange. So, when exchange occurs, new value is created. If people are acting rationally in the exchange, they are both better off. Whether it is trading candy in the exercise described above, or trading wheat, tires, or cotton across an international market, trade creates value that did not exist prior to the trade.

Comparative Advantage

This leads us to a second dimension under the concept of exchange, relating to our giftedness. We all have various skills, talents, and abilities endowed to us by God. Moreover, the development of our creative capacities allows us to specialize in certain productive work (medicine, art, teaching, and agriculture, for example). When we maximize our skills and use them to their best and most productive potential, we are said to have what economists call comparative advantage. To have comparative advantage for a specific skill or trade does not necessarily mean that I can do it better than anyone else. Rather, it means that my costs for doing it are less than someone else trying to do it.

To provide an example, imagine that I have a passion and skill for producing chairs, while my neighbor's giftedness concerns his ability to fish. Both of us can make chairs, and both of us can fish. Yet in one day's work, the number of fish I catch is far less than the number of chairs I can produce. My neighbor is the opposite: the number of fish he catches is far greater than the number of chairs he can produce. We can each try to do both (since we both value chairs and fish), but we each have comparative advantage in our respective areas.

Further, as long as comparative advantage exists, that is, as long as specialization in productive activity differs among members of society, we can gain by trading from one another. In the example above, if I focus specifically on making chairs, and my neighbor devotes all of his time and attention to catching fish, we can trade with one another and gain much more of the chairs and fish we desire than we could if we tried to do both activities ourselves. Specialization, coupled with trade, leads to growth.

Conclusion

To summarize, in co-creating with God, our work should reflect holy and interdependent love that aims to bring abundant life to others. One particular means of seeking and receiving the common good can be realized in entrepreneurial activity, and specifically, what we have described here as social entrepreneurship.

Through the practice of mutually beneficial exchange, and the use of our God-given talents that create specialization, we can achieve important Christian ends such as interdependent growth, participation, and mutually edifying activity.

Naturally, for people of faith, the creation of value should appeal to us. An open marketplace affords individuals the opportunity to partner with one another through the production and exchange of products and services. Yet, in addition to creating additional benefit, it recognizes that others can be a source of value and fulfillment in a given social setting.

This does not mean that free trade is a "Christian slogan" as theologian David Atkinson (1995, 118) has warned. Moreover, conditions allowing for exchange relationships alone are not sufficient to bring about the kingdom ends described above. Nevertheless, our creative action and productive work as humans created in God's image allows us to harness certain exchange and trade arrangements in a redemptive manner. Central to this action is our aim toward a given social mission and a focus upon social and spiritual value creation (not simply economic value).

Discussion Questions

1. The chapter begins by arguing that we are created to work. How does this differ from the notion of toil?

2. The chapter highlights Wesley's famous quote, "The Gospel of Christ knows of no religion, but social; no holiness but social holiness." How does this redefine personal holiness and what is the relationship to our productive activity?

3. What does our work look like if we remove its relational, interdependent dimension? Where do we see this occur in today's contemporary marketplace?

4. When you think about your work, where can you harness certain exchange and trade arrangements in a redemptive manner?

5. Consider your skills, talents, abilities, and passion. Where do you have comparative advantage? How can this advantage be put to use to love God and neighbor?

Works Cited

Atkinson, David J. 1995. "Economic Ethics." In D. J. Atkinson & D. F. Field, eds. *New Dictionary of Christian Ethics and Pastoral Theology*. Downers Grove, IL: IVP Academic.

Crouch, Andy. 2013. *Playing God: Redeeming the Gift of Power*. Downers Grove, IL: InterVarsity Press.

Gutenson, Charles. 2011. *Christians and the Common Good: How Faith Intersects with Public Life*. Grand Rapids, MI: Brazos Press.

Nelson, Tom. 2011. *Work Matters: Connecting Sunday Worship to Monday Work*. Wheaton, IL: Crossway.

Wesley, John, and Charles Wesley. 1739. *Hymns and Sacred Poems*. In *The Works of John Wesley*, 14 vols. Grand Rapids, MI: Zondervan Publishing House, 1958.

Wynkoop, Mildred Bangs. 1972. *A Theology of Love: The Dynamic of Wesleyanism*. Kansas City, MO: Beacon Press.

CHAPTER THREE

WHAT WESLEYAN SOCIAL ENTREPRENEURSHIP LOOKS LIKE

*Kevin Brown, Kevin Kinghorn,
and Tapiwa Mucherera*

As indicated in chapter 1, *social* entrepreneurship begins with identifying a social need. Stemming from the theological discussion of chapter 2, we can summarize a second hallmark of social entrepreneurship. It addresses the social need in a way that, as people's needs are met, they are enabled to work toward meeting the needs of others—a theme that is inherently Wesleyan.

Examples from Wesley's Life

John Wesley undertook a wide variety of projects during his life that exemplify these two hallmarks of social entrepreneurship. He started schools for the education of underprivileged children; built retirement homes for clergymen; established a publishing house that provided theology books and curriculum materials for church groups; and he wrote and printed simple medical guides, distributing them to preachers for the holistic care of their parishioners. These ventures were conceived out of a concern for others followed by subsequent attempts to meet their needs. And as people's needs were met, they, in turn, were better equipped to meet the needs of others.

Wesley is, of course, not alone in undertaking projects that characterize our first two hallmarks of social entrepreneurship: beginning with a social need; and meeting that need in a way that enables others to contribute meaningfully in interdependent relationships. But Wesley did add a distinct feature to the economic projects he initiated. And a Wesleyan engagement in social entrepreneurship will need to consider this feature very carefully.

Wesley's Concern

During the last few years of Wesley's life, he became very concerned with how Methodists would view money in the future. In a tract titled *Thoughts Upon Methodism*, published a few years before he died, Wesley reflected: "Religion necessarily produces both industry and frugality. These virtues always produce wealth" (Kinghorn 2014, 235). The early Methodists in particular, Wesley observed, "in every place grow diligent and frugal, and accordingly they increase in possessions" (Kinghorn 2014, 235). In itself, an accumulation of wealth through honest industry is no bad thing.

However, Wesley saw a great danger in the future wealth that upright, hardworking Methodists would naturally acquire. He forewarned, "I fear that wherever riches have increased, . . . the essence of religion . . . has decreased in the same degree. . . . As wealth increases, so will pride, anger, and the love of the world in all its features" (Kinghorn 2014, 234–5).

Accordingly, Wesley's sermons in the final years of his life were filled with advice and warnings about the handling of money. These sermons include "The Danger of Riches" (1780); "On God's Vineyard" (1787); and, in the last sermon he published, "The Danger of Increasing Riches" (1790). Throughout his life, Wesley had encouraged Methodists to develop virtues, which naturally led them to gain and to save money. Late in his life, he asked repeatedly, "What way can we take so that our money will not sink us into the nethermost hell?" He answered: "There is one way only, and there is no other under heaven: If those who gain all they can, and save all they can, will likewise *give* all they can" (Kinghorn 2014, 235).

A Wesleyan Distinctive

Wesley's unique contribution was not only to *identify* the danger of business projects aimed at the single goal of one's own wealth accumulation, Wesley provided an inspired *remedy* in the form of a system of Christian accountability groups. Methodists were required to participate in societies (community-wide meetings), classes (up to twelve people), and bands (groups of five to six). Mutual accountability was a central element within these groups, including accountability for one's personal finances and business activity. Thus, what is distinctive about Wesleyan social entrepreneurship is this: business ventures are coupled with participation within a rigorous system of mutual accountability to Wesley's exhortation to "Gain all you can; save all you can; give all you can" (Wesley 1872).

In sum, these are the three hallmarks of social entrepreneurship in the Wesleyan spirit: (1) we begin by identifying some social need, following the leading of God; (2) we meet that need in a way that enables others to contribute meaningfully in interdependent relationships; and (3) we participate in some identifiable method of mutual accountability to other Christians for our entrepreneurial practices. There are modern-day examples of social entrepreneurship that embody these three hallmarks. And they demonstrate just how exciting the possibilities can be for positive social change in our world.

When the Indian Ocean tsunami (2004), Hurricane Katrina (2005), and the Haitian earthquake (2010) occurred, people from other communities went to the affected communities and intervened to help as much as they could. There was not a lot of consultation with those who lived in the communities since the immediate needs were known: rescuing people from roof-tops and/or collapsed buildings; providing fresh, clean water and food; ferrying people to dry land; and cleaning up debris. The primary concern initially was the physical safety of those affected and making sure their basic day-to-day needs were met.

These are examples of circumstances that call for short-term intervention to pull people out of danger, so as to be able to come up with long-term solutions. Short-term solutions that are used for long-term purposes are equivalent to applying a Band-Aid to a deep wound. With this in mind, the following example is meant to illustrate a long-term successful project established in a collaborative nature. Among other things, this example reflects Wesley's concern for meeting individual needs and empowering those in need in such a way as to allow them to contribute and participate in community.

Establishing Transformative Social Entrepreneur Projects

Entrepreneurial projects that are meant to be socially transfor-mative are best established collaboratively. As mentioned, one of the first steps with socially transformative projects is to identify a social need. The key leaders of the community (insiders) have

to be on the forefront in this identification process. That is, identifying the need and naming the experience requires proximity.

In 1996, I went to Zimbabwe and visited a parish I had
previously pastored in 1986. One of my former youth members
from that parish had become the pastor, the late Rev. Passwell
Chitiyo. He was excited to see me, and told me of the pressing
need of orphans in the community. The pastor had already
conducted a needs-assessment study and collected data (with
the help of some of the teachers from the local schools) on children and youth in the area that were orphaned due to HIV/
AIDS. The pastor had six local churches in radius of about sixty
kilometers. In this area alone, they had identified approximately two hundred orphans ranging from the ages of about
two to eighteen. The majority of the children were school age,
either living alone or with a relative. Several of the children
came from child-headed families, with children as young as
twelve acting as heads of households. In a handful of the cases,
one parent had died and the other was on their deathbed, dying
from the illness.

The needs were abundant. However, those who worked
and lived in the community understood the nature of these
needs. For example, some of the women in the community
had come together with the pastor to find ways to support
the orphaned children, but did not have the financial means
to provide the necessary help. They had planned to help the
orphans start gardens, raise chicken, goats, or similar projects,
and then use these as means to self-sustain but there was no
capital to finance these planned projects.

Projects that are viable and sustainable are ones that are
usually identified by the community since it is easier for the
community to buy into the idea of the project than people
from outside coming in and identifying the need for those in
the community. Projects brought in from the outside without

communal input will likely die if the community people never catch the vision or get excited about the project (no matter how good or expensive the project may be). Transformative social entrepreneur projects are driven by the desire to not only address needs, but to empower people. This helpful saying is familiar to many: "If you give a man a fish, you feed him for a day; if you teach him how to fish, then you feed him for a lifetime." The man who has learned to fish, will fish from the lakes and dams in his community, thereby using resources readily available to him. Social entrepreneurs add, "If you teach a man how to build fishing poles, then this business will empower an entire community." If he then develops a business to construct fishing poles, he creates jobs in the community that empower the entire community to be fed. Providing people with the means to continue to be self-sufficient and self-sustaining after the missionaries have left is a successful definition of a life-transforming social entrepreneur project.

The pastor shared with me their plans and goals to address the needs identified by the community: "To mobilize resources for sustainability through the introduction of the projects like grinding mills, poultry, piggery, etc.; assist orphans spiritually, morally, materially and train them survival skills so to be self-reliant; to economically empower the women-volunteer caregivers through training and assisting them start their own income generating projects like tie and dye; to reduce the menace of HIV/AIDS through workshops and education and encouraging behavioral change (Musodza and Chitiyo 1999, 2). One of the things attributed to Mahatma Gandhi is that he said: "Poverty is the worst form of violence. Anyone who has dealt with poverty knows how expensive it is." I would add that poverty and HIV/AIDS are a deadly combination that is worse than some wars throughout human history. The pastor's plan was ambitious. However, he revealed a vision of a community that was ready to fight poverty and disease, and moreover, empower and restore those within the area to be active participants in everyday community life.

Establishment of a Social Entrepreneur Project

Convinced that a holistic approach in caring for the orphans was what was needed to address their physical needs, and knowing the predicament of many of the orphans in Zimbabwe in 1997, I led a mission trip from St. Luke's United Methodist in Highlands Ranch, Colorado, of twenty-three people to Chitimbe in Murewa (Mucherera 2009, 104). We purchased a grinding mill and helped construct the building to house the mill. We worked together with the locals and formed a synergistic partnership to help the orphans in the community. Uzumba Orphan Trust became a model for many communities on how to support orphans in their environment without moving them to orphanages. The main goal was to establish community-based care for the orphans. When we departed from Zimbabwe, we left the Uzumba community with a grinding mill to support approximately three hundred orphaned children. We left more than two thousand dollars as the start-up amount for diesel and repairs for the mill. The group also left clothing that was distributed to the orphans.

This was not a plan where people from Colorado came and left a project in a community without the community's input and involvement. Rather, the community identified the problem and mapped out what they needed to successfully run the project in terms of funds and human resources. Furthermore, they provided whatever resources they could: brick, mortar, water, sand, workforce, and the land to build the housing for the grinding mill. They did not come to watch the American builders and carpenters erect the building. Rather, the local builders and carpenters from the community took the lead in the construction of the mill house. The orphans who would benefit from the project helped in the construction work and we built lasting relationships through this collaborative work.

This project was so successful that it caught the attention of several different organizations. The Uzumba Orphan Trust became the model of an economic endeavor that had far-reaching implications in changing the lives of the orphans of many communities. Joey Butler, who works with the General Board of Global Ministries said, "With the establishment of the grinding mill, the Uzumba Orphan Trust project attracted the attention of UNICEF, Southern African AIDS Trust, SAT, the General Board of Global ministries and many other NGOs as a model program to support the children orphaned by HIV/AIDS. The vision from this project grew and spread around the whole country of Zimbabwe" (Butler 2000, 28; see also Rose 2007, 27; and General Board of Global Ministries of the United Methodist Church).

In 2003, similar projects were established at Gwese UMC, near Mutare and Chibuwe UMC. By 2006 four more grinding mills were bought for Fairfield Orphanage, Bindura UMC, Murombedzi, and Mhakwe. The leaders of these projects at Fairfield, Murombedzi, and Gwese ran the projects to full capacity, and communities are still being impacted to this day.

Successes and Challenges

One of the biggest challenges for these types of projects is the continual change in pastoral leadership. Some of these communities have had pastors appointed to them who were not invested in supporting the projects. Unfortunately, this slowed down the project's momentum. Regrettably, two of the grinding mills were never established because of a change in pastoral leadership. In these two cases, the pastors put a plan together and worked with the community to receive the grinding mill but were relocated before the project was established. Moreover, the next pastors who were appointed lacked passion and/or did not have the know-how and predictably did not follow through with establishing the project.

These challenges aside, the aforementioned projects have been very successful and continue to be life-transforming, with the care mothers and children being supported through the use of the grinding mill profits. Again, the key to these projects is that they are taken upon and received by the communities as their own. Even with the change of pastors, if the project is already established, those in the community will operate the initiative. These projects not only change individual lives, but the whole community is given a sense self-worth and pride in something that they can call their own.

Conclusion

This chapter has sought to provide a more holistic approach to social entrepreneurship and the desire to enact positive social change. As Wesley proposed, the theological impetus for a social venture is not simply identifying and addressing a social need, but seeking to empower and enable the needy in a way that contributes to interdependent and relational love, community participation, and the affirmation of human dignity—the latter of which is cultivated and refined through accountability mechanisms and measures.

The example provided of the Zimbabwe orphan project embodies this holistic approach. The project began with the local pastor conducting a needs-assessment within their community. After identifying the need and naming the forces that served to marginalize vulnerable community members, local members identified a number of high-impact mini-projects that were both viable and sustainable that could affect positive change and, moreover, could be owned by the local community. After the community identified the problem, they partnered with outside groups to bring in resources and material (such as a grinding mill) to realize some of their initiatives. The final outcome was a profit-based venture model that was not only sustainable, but provided the assistance needed to restore vulnerable members of society into full participants.

This story, in many ways, is very redemptive. There is one important caveat to this distinct approach worth reflecting on. For Wesley, an entrepreneurial venture that was social in nature was not motivated simply out of a sense of altruism or social-contract equality. Rather, his motivation was much deeper. In his *Explanatory Notes Upon the New Testament*, Wesley wrote the following with respect to the Gospel of Luke, "With an honest openness of mind, let us always remember the kindred between man and man, and cultivate that happy instinct whereby, in the original constitution of our nature, God has strongly bound us to each other" (Wesley 1818, 174).

In other words, human beings do not simply choose relationship or affiliation; rather, it is within our DNA. We are "relationally constituted" as Wesley put it. God created us for relationship. This has implications for how we consider the idea of social entrepreneurship. Ventures, projects, or initiatives that are social in nature are animated not simply out of a sense of altruistic help. God has designed us in such a way that our own liberation and wholeness is oddly bound up in the restoration, support, and love of others.

Discussion Questions

1. What do you think are the main ingredients of a successful social entrepreneurship project?

2. Can you think of examples of successful social entrepreneurship projects you have seen in your community? Where do we see social ventures today that are successful in some regards, but lacking in a more holistic approach? Is there a common theme?

3. The end of the chapter quotes Wesley and his belief that we are "relationally constituted." How does this change our approach in entrepreneurial ventures? Where do you see this missing today? Where do you see it present?

4. Are there charitable projects in your community that might move more toward self-sustaining enterprises in which all people contribute interdependently? What would need to happen to facilitate that shift?

5. Do you discuss your own business ventures and general monetary practices within the kind of accountability small group that Wesley identified as crucial for our spiritual growth? If not, what next steps might God be calling you to take toward joining or starting such a group?

Works Cited

Butler, Joey. 2000. "It Really Does Take a Village: Uzumba Orphan Trust Keeps AIDS Orphans in Their Own Homes," *Interpreter.* (November–December): 28.

General Board of Global Ministries of the United Methodist Church. n. d. *Zimbabwe HIV-AIDS, Advance #3021529.* http://www .umcmission.org/Give-to-Mission/Search-for-Projects/Projects /3021529.

Kinghorn, Kenneth Cain, ed. 2014. *John Wesley on Methodism.* Lexington, KY: Emeth Press.

Mucherera, Tapiwa. 2009. *Meet Me at the Palaver: Narrative Pastoral Counseling in Postcolonial Contexts.* Eugene, OR: Cascade Books.

Musodza R., and P. Chitiyo. 1999. *Uzumba Orphan Trust: Report for the period of 1998–1999.* Chitimbe, Zimbabwe.

Rose, Laurel L. 2007. *Children's Property and Inheritance Rights, HIV and Aids, and Social Protection in Southern and Eastern Africa.* Working Paper no. 2. HIV/AIDS Programme. Rome: Food and Agriculture Organization of the United Nations and the Norwegian Ministry of Foreign Affairs, 27 section 4.1. ftp://ftp.fao.org/docrep/fao /010/k1195e/k1195e00.pdf.

Wesley, John. 1818. *Explanatory Notes Upon the New Testament.* Fourth American Edition. New York: J Soule and T. Mason for the Methodist Episcopal Church in the United States.

Wesley, John. 1872. *The Use of Money.* Sermon can be accessed from http://www.umcmission.org/Find-Resources /John-Wesley-Sermons/Sermon-50-The-Use-of-Money.

CHAPTER FOUR

FROM A GOOD IDEA TO A GOOD START

W. Jay Moon

Many Americans unknowingly struggle with a very serious disease every day. According to Steve Jobs (Elmer-DeWitt 2011), "it's the disease of thinking that a really great idea is ninety percent of the work." We've all had good, maybe even brilliant, ideas but unless we have execution behind the ideas they slowly wither away as unrealized dreams. You may have heard the saying, "the idea is worth one dollar, but the execution is worth one million."

Consider the example of Emily[1], twenty-two years old, who had a great idea to change the world. She grew up in Ghana, West Africa, and never could forget her experiences there or the people she met. During her undergraduate studies in marketing with a minor in clothing design, she realized a huge opportunity to improve the lives of women at risk in West Africa by employing and training them to sew clothing. Partnering with her close friend Kelsey, she developed creative designs for women's dresses, using the beautiful fabrics that are unique and exclusive to Ghana. It was a great idea, women empowering women through the creation of jobs via beautiful clothing. The idea was exciting, even inspiring, but she was quickly overwhelmed as she realized the amount of logistics involved.

The period of time between a good idea and a good start is extremely dangerous. A lot of ideas are plagued with discouragement, doubt, and a loss of confidence. How does one begin to move from a good idea to a good business start? This chapter describes how to set the groundwork for starting a business with the goal of creating social change.

Innovation Process

Innovation occurs when you see the same thing as others but think different thoughts (von Oech 2008). While there is no guaranteed procedure to follow for successful entrepreneurship, there are successful pathways one can follow. One thing that you can count on, regardless of the situation, is an initial period of uncertainty and doubt. The genesis of the idea prompts the person to depart from the norm, which means there are more questions than answers. This presents an opportunity to rely upon God.

Instead of regarding this as a hard science, innovations are also an art form. This period of the unknown is often a ripe ground for creativity, flexibility, and even playfulness. In his book, *A Whack on the Side of the Head,* Dr. Roger von Oech (2008) differentiates "soft thinking" from "hard thinking" in the following table:

Soft Thinking *(early on)*	Hard Thinking *(later on)*
Metaphor	Logic
Dream	Reason
Humor	Precision
Ambiguity	Consistency
Play	Work
Approximate	Exact
Fantasy	Reality
Paradox	Direct
Diffuse	Focused
Hunch	Analysis
Generalization	Specific
Child	Adult

For the social entrepreneur to innovate and introduce a new idea, they often rely upon soft thinking, especially in the early stages. Later on, hard thinking will result in detailed business planning (the subject of the next chapter). Skipping the soft-thinking phases and rushing to hard thinking may stifle the innovative process and inhibit ingenuity and imagination.

Other terms for soft thinking are "lateral thinking" (De Bono 1968) or "divergent thinking." Instead of finding the one perfect answer to a particular problem, divergent thinking reflects on various combinations and perspectives to identify several right answers. Soft (divergent) thinkers may consider, "How many uses are there for a paper clip?" or "What are the similarities between a cat and a refrigerator?" While this may appear frivolous, the exercise demonstrates an important skill; take the time to answer these questions before reading on. The exercise points out that there are many possible answers to both questions. For example, von Oech describes how a cat and refrigerator both: have a tail, purr, are good places to contain fish and milk, and come in a variety of colors. This type of thinking can stir the innovation process as social entrepreneurs address social problems. While soft thinking can begin the innovation process, von Oech observed that innovators often proceed through various phases to move from a good idea to a good start.

Innovation Phases

While innovation phases do not need to be sequential, von Oech recommends the following approach to develop innovative solutions:

- *Get and Stay Motivated.* God desires people to live in shalom; yet, we often fail to experience this ideal due to human sin. Get and stay motivated by reflecting on what could be a better future and how that reflects God's design for humanity. Consider the changes that are brought upon a community and how circumstances provide windows for improvement. Suppose every problem is really an opportunity, and then reflect on how God may have placed you with specific gifts/abilities/networks to address these opportunities.
- *Search for Insight.* Dig deeply into your own area of experience/expertise. Then, combine this with insights from other disciplines of study. Look for assets in a community and not simply the problems. Emily, for example, combined the study of marketing with clothing design to open new markets for women in Africa, utilizing the assets the women possessed (beautiful fabric, sewing talent, and the ability to teach others). Often, insights arise from being attentive to conversations and observations around you, as you connect the dots.

- *Manipulate Ideas.* Step around assumptions by questioning them. Ask what-if questions, such as, "If we did this, what would happen?" Use manipulation verbs to play with disparate ideas (enlarge, eliminate, combine, adapt, or reverse, for example). A metaphor can unlock fresh insight when you get stuck.

- *Incubate Thoughts.* Move away from the problem and allow the ideas to percolate, like a good brew of coffee. Allow some time for relaxation so that new thoughts can spring forth. While people have various times of high creativity, some of the most fertile venues for innovation include: dreams, exercise, meditation/prayer, long car drives, showering/bathing, late night, or early morning. Find your own creative zone for incubation to occur, and linger there.

- *Illuminate Opportunity.* This is where you begin to visualize the end result. Based on what you have already experienced, ask yourself, *What could be a better future?* Keep a can-do attitude. The majority of innovation comes from dogged persistence. Many contemporary social entrepreneurs experience periods of frustration and have to rely upon persistence by focusing on the end goal. Some would call it stubbornness.

- *Evaluate Proposals.* Once soft thinking is conducted, social entrepreneurs begin to move toward hard thinking. The advice of mentors and other stakeholders can be very helpful. When evaluation is conducted too early, it can stifle the innovation process. On the other hand, the lack of evaluation eventually inhibits action. There comes a time when social entrepreneurs must act upon the information they have at hand. Contemporary social entrepreneurs usually act in small ways, which eventually leads to larger actions that you cannot anticipate.

- *Act on the Best Proposal.* Do not be afraid to fail. If you have done the due diligence, then step out in the direction that seems best. Many contemporary social entrepreneurs experience some failures along the way that become a stepping-stone to later success. Amar Bhide (1999, 84), a business professor who has studied entrepreneurship and innovation for more than twenty years, noted: "businesses cannot be launched like space shuttles, with every detail of the mission planned in advance. . . . Entrepreneurs should play with and explore ideas, letting their strategies evolve through a seamless process of guesswork, analysis, and action."

Contemporary Social Entrepreneurs

To gather advice and identify keys for successful social entrepreneurs, Orlando Rivera and I conducted field research on seven contemporary social entrepreneurs. Their social contexts included Native American reservations, a Muslim city in Ghana, a poor coal-mining town in Kentucky, and New York City downtown neighborhoods. They all combined ministry in local churches with their business in the neighborhoods. We visited their business settings, read their publications, and interviewed them to identify how they went from a good idea to a good start. Here are some general observations gathered from these successful social entrepreneurs:

Initial Motivation

* *Identify the Need*. They all recognized an area that was lacking or needed improvement and wanted to make a change. For most, they were dissatisfied with the status quo, while others had a desire to reverse circumstances forced upon them due to shifts in the community (such as gentrification of the neighborhood).
* *Wait for God's Direction*. They were willing to move slowly as they waited for God to show further direction, and all went through a time of waiting and prayer. This was a period of

uncertainty where they really did not know exactly what to do next. They felt a strong call by God (motivating them to step out), but the exact steps were not spelled out so they had to depend on God for daily guidance.

- *Embrace Different Experiences.* All had lived in other cultural settings and were willing to move to a new location and take risks. Financial need was sometimes the original motivation, specifically some of the pastors were seeking to support their ministry locally without depending on outside funds. The various cultural experiences fostered new and fresh approaches to nagging problems.

- *Start Where You Are with What You Have.* All of the businesses started off small with very simple steps like making cookies, cutting hedges, building a small building, or selling fish, for example. They used their existing interests, talents, and experiences to build the business (like horseback riding, house construction, or business experience). They found that being faithful in small things led to greater opportunity later.

Personal Background

- *Faith Is the Foundation.* All had a strong and developing Christian faith. They were risk-takers (not impulsive gamblers though), not deterred easily (willing to wait for God's direction), a bit stubborn (not deterred by initial failure or later opposition from the church or community), and they had previous experience in ministry before launching their social entrepreneurship.

- *Those Closest to Us Become Our Strongest Assets.* They all had connections with outside partners who later came alongside them to assist. One surprise that I found was that most of the social entrepreneurs had a spouse with significant business experience. Several described how they relied upon their spouse for daily business such as operations, finance, or accounting. Funding sources also usually came from a close network of friends, family members, coworkers, church members, and larger church connections. Howard Dayton, founder of Crown Ministries and Compass ministry, is adamant that those who are contemplating a business start-up should seek a mentor. He warned, "it's imperative that you pray for the Lord to send you a mentor. This can mean the difference between success and failure" (Dayton 2014, 33). In fact, Thomas Cooney (2005, 226–27), professor of entrepreneurship at the Dublin Institute of Technology, researched successful entrepreneurs and observed, "One of the great myths of entrepreneurship has been the notion of the entrepreneur as a lone hero . . . the reality is that successful entrepreneurs either built teams about them or were part of a team throughout."

Community Change

♦ *Positive Change Restores Relationships.* The businesses that were created would all eventually result in an increase in social capital and goodwill with community leaders and the general population. In some cases, these businesses created trust between the church and community where mistrust previously existed. Because the businesses employed local people and often used the additional profit to support further ministry efforts, a channel of mutual benefit and connection was created.

♦ *Prepare to Move Lunch Tables.* Some of the businesses opened channels for people who did not formerly interact with each other (like cowboys and Indians sharing a meal together). The social entrepreneurship became a bridge to allow others who lived outside of the context to participate in the social change process. For example, outside churches often came to visit and help.

Ministry Results

◆ *Use Business to Grow Ministry*. Some of the businesses funded
new church planters' salaries. The businesses also encouraged other local churches to grow, bring different churches
together for common discussions, and help the community
see the church as a benefit to the community, especially in
areas where there was suspicion (such as Muslim contexts).
The businesses allowed the pastors to interact with wider
influential networks in society (like bankers, town council
members, mayors, and other local leaders). This allowed
their ministry to become self-supporting and not dependent
on outside assistance. One pastor noted how he now felt free
to voice his real opinions and set his own course for ministry
without outside interference. This is particularly important
for a cross-cultural ministry.

Cross-Cultural Change

Social entrepreneurs often address social concerns in other
cultures, which add another layer of complexity. It's easy to
recognize an injustice occurring in another culture and wish
there was something you could do to fix it, but how many
people have actually sparked a movement that rectifies the
injustice? Cross-cultural social change does not come easily or
quickly, and it's important for social entrepreneurs to understand how it typically occurs.

Anthropologist Everett Rogers (2003) researched the change
process in cultures around the world described in his classic text,
Diffusion of Innovations. Rogers observed that cultural change is
always occurring but it usually starts on the margins of society.
People often assume that change commences at the center of
power (with the president, CEO, or pastor, for example). The
problem is that people in the center of power often have too

much to lose if the innovation fails. It would require risking their credibility, status, income, and even their very jobs. As a result, those at the center of power are often a conservative force to minimize change. Maintaining their own position is of the upmost importance, as there is little danger involved with keeping things the way they are. Rogers observed that real change in society usually starts with those on the margins, which, for most of us, is good news. History reveals that those without wealth and formal positions of power often become change agents to make a difference.

Change Agents

Change agents are often on the margins of society and hover between two cultures. Rogers (2003, 336) stated, "the change agent is a marginal figure with one foot in each of two worlds." They have developed a deep understanding and passion for both cultures but do not get blinded by the ethnocentrism of one culture alone.

For instance, in the example at the beginning of this chapter, Emily's background as a missionary kid suits her well to be a change agent. Living nine years of her life in a remote West African village, she saw how African women lived and struggled every day. She also observed their hard work, interpersonal ability, and beautiful clothing worn on festive occasions. Returning to the United States to complete her schooling, it took ten years of American culture immersion before Emily's idea sparked in her mind. Deep engagement and understanding of two cultures is essential in order to effectively balance between the two.

While change agents live deeply in both cultures, the continual suspension between the two creates an internal limbo in which they never quite find themselves totally at home in either one. This tension provides a fertile ground for change agents to connect ideas from both cultures in order to introduce change. Opportunities for cross-cultural experiences are plentiful even inside the United States, such as someone from rural Kentucky moving to urban Lexington, Kentucky.

Along with a multicultural background, anthropologist and missiologist Charles Kraft (1996, 388) identified the following common characteristics of change agents:

+ Respected or prestigious
+ Authentic and sincere
+ Enthusiastic or aggressive (in the sense that they are willing to extend themselves and suffer for it, if necessary)
+ Able to influence opinion leaders
+ Committed to long-term, extended contact
+ Friendliness of contact

Potential social entrepreneurs should consider this list of characteristics to see if they identify with these traits. It's very uncommon for one person to posses all of these elements. Change agents typically identify partners (in the form of their spouse, friends, or family members) to work with who can complement these traits. Change agents must form partnerships with strategic individuals, particularly inside innovators.

Inside Innovators

Rogers found that change agents have a limited role. Change agents often act as the facilitators of a new idea or concept but they need people inside the culture who can innovate and adapt the idea. For example, while Emily can introduce an idea to African women, innovators *inside* African culture need to adapt this idea to fit their local context. Aspiring social entrepreneurs should take note. Your role is to present your idea to a cultural insider who can then innovate and adapt this concept.

Emily returned to Ghana, West Africa, to introduce her idea. Building on relationships that she and her family had previously established, she identified two seamstresses that were skilled in sewing and willing to adapt Emily's ideas to work within the Ghanaian culture. She resourced the seamstresses with sewing machines and oversaw the production of twenty dresses.

Finding the right innovators is *crucial* to success. In order to guide the search to find the right innovators, Kraft (1996, 388) provided the following set of characteristics:

- Feeling a need for change (they are themselves in tension or transition)
- Open to change
- Free to pursue change
- Believe change is possible and advisable
- Desire to gain personally (for example, economically, spiritually, or through social prestige or power)
- Literate (introducing them to ideas from afar)

Social entrepreneurs realize that working with innovators is a key to the change process; therefore, they take their time to identify those that meet the above criteria. In addition to innovators, there is one other category of person that Rogers found was key to the innovation process: early adopters.

Early Adopters

Early adopters are not like the rest of society. While the majority of American women are not willing to experiment with new fashion designs, a small percentage (Rogers (2003, 262) estimates early adopters are around 13.5 percent of the population) are willing to take a risk and adopt a new idea. These people are crucial to the change process. Again, the role of the change agent is to identify and then empower these early adopters.

In the American culture, Emily began establishing a market for the dresses by building a brand. This required the development of a social media presence as well as a website that she knew young American women would identify with. She is now looking for young American women who will wear these dresses in public for others to see. If people like what they see in these early adopters, then the idea catches on. Rogers's model predicts that if this new innovation is a good one, then late adopters will come along in time. Eventually, the idea gains momentum and then change reaches the center of power. Perhaps, one day the first lady of the United States will wear one of Emily's dresses! The process, though, usually *starts* on the margins instead of the center. The social entrepreneur who understands and works with this process will find himself or herself on the road to success.

Conclusion

After Emily visited Ghana for a feasibility study, her brother then presented the idea to the Asbury Project for funding. The initial funds were then used to finance operations for the first order of dresses, now for sale at www.bygracedesigns.org. She is still moving ahead with her dream, one dress at a time.

While there is no silver bullet to guarantee success for social entrepreneurs, the concepts outlined above remove some of the mystery to help aspiring social entrepreneurs move from a good idea to a good start. In the next chapter, you will be encouraged to develop a business plan that will help you ask some important detailed questions. Before moving to the next chapter, though, spend some time in soft (divergent) thinking. While necessity may be the mother of invention, the father of invention is often . . . play! (von Oech 2003).

Discussion Questions

1. Think about the last time that you had a really creative idea. Where/when is your most creative zone? Give yourself the freedom to play and linger in that zone.

2. To start your creative juices flowing, play with soft thinking. Can you think of a metaphor that describes your problem? Allow yourself to daydream, fantasize, and ponder hunches. Be childlike by comparing your social problem to something else and then looking for similarities.

3. Practice the innovation phases that von Oech suggests. What stage do you get stuck on? Who might you call on to be a part of your team to help you move forward? If you do not have a good mentor yet, start praying for one.

4. Consider the experiences of the seven contemporary social entrepreneurs discussed in the chapter. Do you see anything in your own story that connects with the way God worked in their lives? What can you learn from their experiences to guide you?

5. What is the perceived problem that you are addressing and what assets exist already in the culture that you are trying to influence? This moves you away from getting overwhelmed by the problem and starting to look for possible evidence of God's prevenient grace already in the culture. For further help, consider the "appreciative inquiry" process (Hammond 2013).

Works Cited

Bhide, Amar. 1999. "How Entrepreneurs Craft Strategies That Work." In *Harvard Business Review on Entrepreneurship*: 57–88. Boston, MA: Harvard Business School Publishing.

Cooney, Thomas M. 2005. "Editorial: What Is an Entrepreneurial Team?" *International Small Business Journal* 23 (3): 226–35.

Dayton, Howard. 2014. *Business God's Way*. Orlando, FL: Compass.

De Bono, Edward. 1968. *New Think: The Use of Lateral Thinking in the Generation of New Ideas*. New York: Basic Books.

Elmer-DeWitt, Philip. 2011. "Steve Jobs: The Parable of the Stones." *Fortune*, November 11. http://fortune.com/2011/11/11/steve-jobs-the-parable-of-the-stones/.

Hammond, Sue Annis. 2013. *The Thin Book of Appreciative Inquiry*. Third Edition. Thin Book Series. Bend, OR: Thin Book Publishing.

Kraft, Charles H. 1996. *Anthropology for Christian Witness*. Maryknoll, New York: Orbis.

Rogers, Everett M. 2003. *Diffusion of Innovations*. Fifth edition. NY: Free Press.

von Oech, Roger. 2008. *A Whack on the Side of the Head: How You Can Be More Creative*. Lebanon, IN: Grand Central Publishing.

Note

1. While this chapter mentions Emily alone, her longtime friend, Kelsey, and her brother, Josh, have assisted her. I will use Emily's name throughout the article, though, as a composite character that represents the contributions of this team.

For Further Study

The following DVDs by Acton Media are recommended for further study, reflection, and discussion on the entrepreneurship process:

2011. *The Call of the Entrepreneur,* DVD. http://www.callofthe entrepreneur.com/.

2012. *Poverty Cure,* DVD Series. http://www.povertycure.org.

2014. *For the Life of the World,* DVD Series. http://www.letterstothe exiles.com/.

CHAPTER FIVE

GETTING STARTED WITH SOCIAL ENTREPRENEURSHIP
HOW TO WRITE A BUSINESS PLAN

David Bosch, Kevin Brown, and Mark Gill

Starting with a Problem

Here's a question: What do Matt and Jessica Flannery, founders of Kiva Microfinance, have in common with Takeru Kobayashi, the famed competitive eater who once scarfed down sixty-nine hot dogs in just ten minutes?

At first glance, it would seem that the two would have very little in common. However, both provide examples of what it means to possess an entrepreneurial spirit. First, both identified a problem. For the Flannerys, it was stagnant poverty in developing countries. For Kobayashi, it was moving the bar for competitive hot dog consumption. Second, both redefined the nature of the problem. Kobayashi stopped asking, "How do I eat more hot dogs?" and asked a new question: "How do I make hot dogs easier to eat?" (Levitt and Dubner 2014). Similarly, the Flannerys recognized that poverty had less to do with the incapacity of the impoverished, and more to do with their lack of access to capital markets (Kiva n.d.). Finally, after identifying the problem and redefining the nature of that problem, both engaged in implementation. For the Flannerys, this ultimately led to micro lending. For Kobayashi, it led to an innovative, and painfully methodical, approach to consuming hot dogs (and a lot more calories!).

Undoubtedly, implementation could not occur without the recognition of an initial problem. Entrepreneurial thinking has always concerned itself with creatively addressing existing problems, gaps, and limitations in the marketplace. In other words, entrepreneurs see opportunity where others may not. This has implications for those who concern themselves with social problems. In particular, people of faith are called to have an eye toward the marginalized members of society. Indeed, to "bear one another's burdens" is to fulfill the "law of Christ" (Gal. 6:2 NRSV).

Combining an opportunistic head with a socially minded heart is, as we have argued, at the very center of social entrepreneurship. However, identifying a problem and an innovative solution will mean little if you don't have a disciplined strategy for implementation. For new ventures, implementation should begin with a business plan. Entrepreneur Guy Kawasaki, in discussing the value of a business plan, wrote, "All the late-night, back-o'-the-envelope, romantic intentions to change the world become tangible and debatable once they're put on paper. Thus, the document itself is not nearly as important as the process that leads to the document. Even if you aren't trying to raise money, you should write one anyway" (Kawasaki 2004, 68).

We are all aware that "the best laid plans of mice and men always go awry." As true as this may be, it is equally true that *failing to plan* is like *planning to fail*. A successful business will always recognize opportunity, customers, and profit potential. All of these areas are given deliberate reflection, analysis, and consideration in a planning document. In other words, issues of failure or success are often fleshed out in the initial business plan!

While an Internet search of a business plan template is likely to produce a variety of different business plan models (see the websites for the Small Business Administration or entrepreneur.com for more details), most, if not all, share a common set of components. The purpose of this chapter is to introduce the reader to these components and their respective content. With this said, please keep in mind that templates cannot produce certain outcomes. For example, a good template cannot create a great idea. Nor can it clearly communicate content. Further, templates cannot convey confidence or even guarantee that your idea will be funded. This aside, if your business plan addresses the items we describe below in a clear, comprehensive manner, we do claim that it is the best way to posture the long-term success of a business. For those aiming to address a social problem or gap (such as poverty, health, or job creation) in a sustainable manner, the business plan is not merely important, but vital.

Part I: Executive Summary

All business plans begin with an executive summary. As the name implies, this provides a comprehensive overview of the entire business plan. Often times, while this is the first section of the business plan, the authors write it last (since it is a descriptive summary). One key component of the executive summary relates to the problem being addressed or the underlying need. In other words, it is describing the nature of the opportunity.

What are the forces creating the opportunity, and the timeliness and size of the opportunity? For example, a remote village may not have the resources at their disposal, given their primitive environment, to create clean drinking water. This obviously creates an array of problems related to health, social structure, and the village's ability to flourish in the future.

Related to the clear statement of opportunity, it is important to effectively communicate up front the products or the services that you are offering in order to capitalize on this opportunity. For example, while clean drinking water has been a problem in the past for this particular village, you may be offering a solution in the form of water tablets, an innovative water-well design, or perhaps a new de-salinization technology.

While the executive summary is presenting the reader with a general description of the business plan (however long it may be), you want to be clear with respect to your product or service and how it relates to the nature of the opportunity. Think about this as the elevator pitch to potential investors. In other words, it is a brief description of your business if you only had the time of an elevator ride to describe your idea.

Part II: The Industry

Not all industries are made alike. Sales in a grocery store are much different than sales in an insurance company. The products, services, manufacturing, and marketing all relate to the nature of the industry you are in. Thus, spelling this out up front is very important. Typically, this section includes information related to the nature of the industry. This may include addressing the industry size (in dollars), the annual growth rate in the industry, key trends (costs, prices, product development, or seasonality, for example), success factors, and standard financial ratios. Industries can be local or global, big or small, new or already in existence. The important point is that you are demonstrating a clear understanding of the environment that you aim to operate within.

Part III: Company, Products, and Services

If your business has been in existence for some time, this is where you will give the reader a brief history of the organization. Additionally, for new and existing organizations you will want to describe to the reader the mission, vision, and values of the organization. This will give the potential investor a deeper understanding of the organization beyond the current business concept.

What is the essence of your business concept? This is an important question, and the answer will ultimately determine the product or service produced and marketed by your venture. This is the section where you say, "Therefore, we are offering _____."

Your service, for example, might be a job-training program. Here, you would describe the program and how it fits with the nature of the opportunity you have already identified. If job training is your service, how will you get started? That is, how will you enter the marketplace? Further, what is your vision over the next six months? Year? Five years?

This section does not necessarily outline the marketing approach. (That is the next section.) It does, however, provide the reader with a clear sense of who you are as a business. That is, your identity and your respective business concept.

Part IV: Competitive Advantage, Market Research, and Analysis

Now that you have described what opportunity it is that you are addressing, and the product or service you are providing, it is important to emphasize the competitive advantage that makes you unique. Some have described this as articulating your unfair advantage. For example, many business-minded persons endeavor to start a restaurant, harvest coffee, or market their handmade crafts. However, this alone is insufficient to make them unique. Therefore, it is very important to both understand and to explain your competitive advantage.

From here, this important section provides specific details into your market research. This is one of the most difficult sections to prepare in the entire business plan; however, it is also one of the most important. Why? Because this is where you show that you know your customers! A business plan, in essence, is a forecast. The marketing section is the appropriate place to actually substantiate the numbers and figures you are forecasting.

A good marketing section will describe the market itself, the size, the customer, and the overall market potential. It will discuss market segmentation, or how the market is broken up into specific groups of interested or relevant customers. (Demographics, psychographics, information sources utilized, or product usage rate can all be useful.) Segmentation is important because it allows you to identify which segments of the market represent the greatest sales potential. For example, a minivan may be marketed broadly to everyone, but the greatest sales potential would be to families who have children.

Market research also involves an understanding of the forces that affect or influence the market. This includes the economy, prices of inputs, policy or legislation, or other influential factors external to the company. Further, understanding your market means understanding your customers, or what is called competitive analysis. Who are your direct competitors? Who are potential competitors? Is the market saturated or open? If it is open, could it be saturated in the future (that is, is your product or service something that can easily be replicated)? Do your competitors offer something that you do not? Conversely, how are you different or unique from your competitors? How do you compare with your competition on quality, price, performance, delivery, timing, service, or warranties (insofar as they are applicable)?

Part V: Economics of the Business

The next section discusses the economics of the business. Here, a good business plan will look at the nature of their expenses. Fixed costs are expenses that will need to be paid whether the company ever sells any products or not. This may include things like utilities, mortgages, insurance, or licensure. Variable costs are the expenses that fluctuate based upon your level of sales. This may include things like commission on sales, direct costs of materials used for the product, or shipping costs. It is important to determine if a great deal of the costs incurred are fixed or variable, and the composition between them. For example, if most of the costs are fixed, then achieving a certain level of sales becomes more important for a venture to sustain itself.

In addition to understanding the nature of the costs, a good business plan will know the margins related to the product or service. In other words, how much money does it cost you to produce the product or service, and how much money are you selling this for. The difference between the two is understood as a margin. Among other things, this section is detailing how the company will make money (revenues exceeding costs). Often times, it is in analyzing and writing out this section of the business plan that companies realize that their model is not financially viable.

This section also includes one of the more important numbers in the entire business plan: the break-even point. This is the point where your income and your expenses literally break-even. For example, if you are selling beads and necklaces that are unique to a particular area, how many units would you need to sell in order to be even with the costs to produce those sales? Typically, the formula to determine the number of units is: $\frac{Fixed\ Costs}{Price\ Per\ Unit\text{---}Variable\ Cost\ Per\ Unit}$

So, we might imagine that our fixed cost to run a business where we sell necklaces is $5,000 per year. Further, imagine that the sales price per necklace is $10 and the variable cost is $4. Our break-even analysis is as follows: $\frac{\$5,000}{\$10\text{--}\$4}$ or about 834 units. To put that in a complete sentence, we would need to sell approximately 834 necklaces in a given year (about 70 per month) in order for the revenues of the business equal to the total costs to operate the business.

Part VI: Market Plan

The market plan section of the business plan, while similar, is different from the competitive analysis and market research section (described in part IV). Specifically, this section of the plan should incorporate an actual marketing strategy. How will you reach your specified target market? That is, how will they know about your product or service? In this section, you will want to provide a schedule with the approximate costs of promotion and advertising and discuss how these costs will be incurred.

This section also deals with one of the more important aspects of the business plan as it relates to your product or service. The price! Not only will you share your price here, but also you will want to share your pricing strategy. The pricing strategy will vary based upon your goal with the business. Are you trying to gain new market share? Maximize profit? Enter a brand new market? Answering these questions will determine your pricing strategy. Specific strategies include: skimming, penetration pricing, parity pricing, sliding price strategy, odd pricing, leader pricing, price lining, price bundling, geographic pricing, discount (seasonal, special group, quantity), and cash discount. (See the American Marketing Association's *Dictionary of Marketing Terms* to better understand these terms.)

In addition to price and price strategy, you will want to cover your distribution channels. Specifically, do you have a supply chain necessary to produce your product or service? If so, who is involved in that? Finally, you will want to provide details around your customer service strategies or warranty policies in this section of the business plan.

Part VII: Social and Spiritual Impact Plan

Much like how it is important to adequately plan for the business aspects of an organization, for a social enterprise it is just as important to plan for the social and spiritual impacts of the organization. One aspect of a social enterprise is the concept of a triple bottom line, or multiple bottom lines. We have already talked about the financial bottom line, so in this section we need to plan for the social and spiritual bottom lines.

The organization needs to clearly articulate the social ill(s) that are being addressed by the enterprise and the social value the organization is going to provide. Both the social ill(s) and the programs that are going to be put in place need to be adequately described.

Finally, just as one can assess the financial bottom line of an organization by calculating its profit, an organization needs a way to assess its social and spiritual impact. To assist in this, this section should include what metrics will be calculated to determine if the enterprise is having an impact. For example, if the organization hopes to address illiteracy rates, then this section would enumerate the impact the enterprise plans to make and how they would go about doing it.

Measuring spiritual impact is more difficult. Much prayer and thought must be done in order to determine what should be measured and how it should be measured. There needs to be humility in those involved in the enterprise as they understand that they cannot usurp or take credit for God working and moving among people. However, a lack of planning for spiritual impact may lead to a lack of spiritual impact. Thus, in this section, the enterprise should clearly identify what spiritual impact they are attempting to have and how they will measure the impact they are having.

Part VIII: Operations Plan

You have now reached the section of the plan where you deal with operations. In essence, this simply covers the processes that deliver your product or service to the customer. If you are producing a product, what is the manufacturing process involved in its production? If supplying a service, you will want to describe the delivery process that is necessary to provide your service. Also, in this section you will want to describe your approach to quality control, production control, and inventory control. Specifically, what quality control and inspection procedures will be used to minimize service problems and associated customer dissatisfaction.

You will want to provide specific details around the equipment required to operate your venture. List the facilities, including plant and office space, storage and land areas, special tooling, machinery, and other equipment needed to conduct business. It is also important to discuss whether equipment and space will be leased or acquired (new or used) and indicate the costs and timing of such actions. How much of the proposed financing will be devoted to plant/equipment?

A very important aspect of the operations plan relates to the geographical location. First, you will want to indicate if the venture does, indeed, have a physical location (or if it is online-based). If physical, this section will include any location analysis or site selection that you have done. You will also want to discuss any advantages or disadvantages of your location in terms of labor availability and your proximity to customers or suppliers. Finally, describe the state and local taxes and if there are any zoning regulations of which to be aware.

Last but not least, your operations section will detail important legal considerations or legal issues that may affect the operation. Does the business require any particular permits? If so, what is your action plan to secure them? As with everything else in the business plan, you are simply showing that you have an awareness of the environment under which you aim to operate.

Part IX: Management Team

This section simply outlines the organizational structure of your business, and offers you an opportunity to elaborate on key figures in the venture, their expertise, and the overall contribution they will make in achieving sustainable success. The section should specifically include information around personnel and their responsibilities, the organizational structure, compensation and ownership, and the background of the key individuals (the relevance of their experience). In addition, describe the immediate, short-term, and long-term staffing needs for the venture and your plans to fulfill them.

Finally, in this section you will want to indicate the names and affiliations of any advisors you have selected to assist or mentor you with respect to the venture (legal advisor, or consultants, for instance). For example, if a missionary who has spent twenty-five years in a third-world environment is consulting you on starting a business there, this would be an appropriate place to include that information.

Part X: Critical Risks and Assumptions

As humans, we have an implicit bias toward optimism. This is often a good thing, but it can be a liability when we are trying to objectively forecast and execute a plan (which is the very nature of the business plan document). Therefore, it is important to have a section of the plan that demonstrates your ability to think carefully about critical risks that threaten the viability or long-term sustainability of your plan. Further, this section allows you to highlight the assumptions you are making (assumptions that play a key role in the success of your plan).

After identifying three to five critical risks and assumptions related to the plan, you will want to offer contingency plans that will allow you to absorb the blow should one of the critical risks you mention come to fruition (or should one of your assumptions fail to hold).

A business plan can be a delicate document because you want to show that you are optimistic about the success of your venture. However, you don't want to be so optimistic that you are blind to the forces that may threaten your venture getting off the ground (or maintaining sustainability). Writing this section well will provide the necessary balance between optimism and blind optimism.

Part XI: The Financial Plan

In this section you will provide some actual numbers related to your finances. Specifically, you will be using pro-forma financial statements, which simply means that they are financial statements based upon future forecasted data, not existing actual data.

Different business plan templates (see the Small Business Administration's website or entrepreneur.com) will suggest different information here, but for the most part, a good financial section will include pro-forma financial statements for at least two years (month-by-month). Specifically, this will include the income statement, balance sheet, and the cash-flow statements. As mentioned, while these numbers are forecasted, the statements should represent your best estimates of the early stages of the venture from a financial standpoint.

Keep in mind that this section is not simply the presentation of numbers. As an author, you will want to highlight important milestones in the statements (like when you break even), the amount of equity or debt needed to start the project, and other important conclusions (for example, "Our start-up costs are as follows . . .").

Finally, you will want to offer a list of any financial assumptions you are making when constructing the financial statements. For example, you may have assumptions about interest rates, partnership agreements, or sales contracts that you will want to highlight to substantiate how you arrived at your numbers.

Part XII: The Proposed Company Offering

The business plan is necessary for many different aspects of starting a new venture or building upon an existing one. One popular usage of the business plan is to secure funding. If this is the case for your venture, then in many ways, you have been leading up to this section. The proposed offering is your opportunity to request the desired amount of money necessary to get started.

Specifically, you will want to indicate the amount of money being sought. If, in return, you are offering ownership in the company, you will want to specify this to the potential investor and include their estimated rate of return. Finally, you will want to emphasize how those investor funds will be spent within the plan (for items such as start-up costs, for example).

Conclusion

Whether it is to secure funding, gain participation, or raise awareness, the primary value of a business plan is to demonstrate an acute understanding, both to yourself *and* to others, of the opportunities, finances, growth, threats, environment, and assumptions relative to your venture.

Discussion Questions

1. What do you think are the common barriers to executing a business plan successfully?
2. This chapter quotes Guy Kawasaki, who said, "The [business plan] itself is not nearly as important as the process that leads to the document." What do you think he means by this?
3. Why should people of faith be just as concerned with planning and technical execution as they are with the identification of problems and the desire to bear the burdens of others?
4. A great body of research has developed over the last several years suggesting that humans tend to possess "confirmation bias"—that is, we interpret evidence in a way that seems to confirm what we already think. Why is this a bias we need to be aware of, particularly as it relates to identifying critical risks and assumptions within the business plan document?
5. What is keeping you, as an entrepreneur, from investing the time and energy into a comprehensive business-planning document to move your venture forward?

Works Cited

Entrepreneur.com. n.d. *Business Plans: A Step by Step Guide.* http://www.entrepreneur.com/businessplan/index.html.

Kawasaki, Guy. 2004. *The Art of the Start: The Time-Tested, Battle-Hardened Guide for Anyone Starting Anything.* New York: Portfolio.

Kiva. n.d. *Kiva: History.* http://www.kiva.org/about/history.

Levitt, Steven D., and Stephen J. Dubner. 2014. *Think Like a Freak extract: joining the dots between hot dogs, Van Halen and David Cameron.* From *Think Like a Freak.* http://www.theguardian.com/books/2014/may/11/think-like-a-freak-extract-steven-levitt-stephen-dubner-van-halen-david-cameron.

Small Business Administration. n. d. *SBA—Writing a Business Plan.* https://www.sba.gov/writing-business-plan.

CHAPTER SIX

CHANGE THE WORLD, BUT NOT ALONE

Russell W. West and Thomas F. Tumblin

*"In organizations, real power and energy is gener-
ated through relationships. The patterns of relationships
and the capacities to form them are more important
than tasks, functions, roles, and positions."*
—MARGARET J. WHEATLEY,
LEADERSHIP AND THE NEW SCIENCE

*"Come to me, all you who are struggling hard and
carrying heavy loads, and I will give you rest. Put
on my yoke, and learn from me. I'm gentle and
humble. And you will find rest for yourselves. My
yoke is easy to bear, and my burden is light."*
—JESUS CHRIST, MATTHEW 11:28–30 (CEB)

Introduction: To Whom Much Is Given . . .

*He knew it was possible. As an ophthalmologist who had done short-
term medical mission trips in numerous countries, he saw the shortages*

of eye surgeons, especially in the rural areas. While there were 16,279 active in the United States in 2009 according to the American College of Surgeons Health Policy Research Institute, there was only a fraction of that in the countries he served. The medical resources of the world are not equitably distributed around the world. In that sense, life is not fair.

But he had an idea, an entrepreneurial idea. He could design a tool that would allow medical professionals in remote areas to perform basic surgical procedures. With adequate training, a surgical nurse could safely care for many of the ophthalmology needs. His device could help level the medical playing field. He found a partner in a lab tech firm. They refined the device to meet the specifications of the experts in the field. After training a network of surgical nurses and medical professionals to perform the procedure, testing of this new medical tool is underway in multiple countries with much success.

We, the authors, have started companies, advised spiritual and social entrepreneurs, and coached congregations into being the most missional they can be with the people entrusted to them. This experience with missional innovators causes us to believe the world yearns for transformation (see Bitzer 1968). The social entrepreneur described in the introduction of this chapter is an example of a typical member of a spiritual community who saw a need and did what made the most sense. And his community followed him into mission. In this respect, this citizen stepped into the activities that have only recently come under the popular technical term "social entrepreneur," a kind of social innovator who leverages opportunities and business disciplines to advance the common good.[2] Our experience has shown lasting transformation is seldom the work of a lone heroic leader with a fixed jaw set against the wind and opposition. Instead, durable change is often generated from faceless and nameless communities of the committed who covenant together to make things different through their joint efforts. In this respect, we imagine congregations as being the kinds of communities that call, cultivate, send, and celebrate creative people in their midst who might be some of God's problem-solvers in a world that earnestly invites transformation. What if God thinks *you* are part of the solution? What if God wants to birth new ideas, technologies, and companies out of something you see that needs to be changed in the world?

In this chapter, we will describe the congregation as a community that cultivates social entrepreneurs, or what we might call *solutionaries*. We discuss some of the solution-creating obstacles, as well as explore partnering as a reflex that causes the good idea of one mature person to become the better ideas for the social good. Last, we will discuss a collaboratory map as a way to take stock of the rich relational resources that might be invited to join the social solution, along with providing a worksheet that lets you get started on cultivating your own community of stakeholders.

From One to Many: When Congregations Cultivate Solutionaries

This is a dramatic story of an ordinary person awakening to an entrepreneurial moment. His local church was not resistant to his ideas. At the same time, the church was not necessarily nurturing the entrepreneur within. For most churches, it is not in their culture to do so. When individuals do catch the passion, the church celebrates them with inspiring warmth. We hope to inspire the church as an igniter of such sparks of passion, solution, and expertise. We hope to see churches return to their historical expertise of innovating missionally for the "common good," making their best ideas matter to the world around them (see Crouch 2012).

In too many congregations, holy experiments rarely emerge. The quiet status quo of a satisfying worship experience amongst friends feels preferable to the radical invitation to step out of the boat. Walking on water is for the crazies. No one in any state of normalcy would expect mere mortals to take such risks. But perhaps we should generate new answers to a series of theological what-if questions, such as:

* What if churches are intended to be incubators rather than inoculators?
* What if God's invitation is to go deep in our personal relationship with Christ and one another for the sake of mission?
* What if we were actually created for good, if at times scary, acts of service?
* What if the church's role is to gestate holy experiments that address needs rather than preserve safety only?

From the days of Adam and Eve, God has intended to engage us in meaningful occupation. The idyllic scene is one of daily transparency with the Creator and a faithful stewardship of creation. Walking openly with God and attending to God's enterprise remains the goal. God entrusts us with a role to play in making the kingdom more visible. While God could save the world without us, God chooses to speak and work through us. The divine turnaround initiated by the birth, death, and resurrection of Jesus Christ means we participate in the unfolding of the new heaven and earth. God's in-breaking kingdom comes, in part, through us. It is still God's kingdom, not ours. It is Christ in us, the hope of glory, not our own doing. Yet, as we join God in mission, regardless of our vocation, our lives are changed as well. Not only do we make a difference in the lives we touch in the name of Christ, we are transformed as well.

All of the various images of the church we find in Scripture call for more than the traditional picture we often have in our minds. While the congregation is to be a place of comfort and encouragement, it is also to be a place of sending. It should be a peaceful sanctuary. It should also be a venue for unnerving challenge. Healthy congregations host dangerous conversations. People alive in their own faith keep hearing the voice of God. Sometimes that voice speaks, "Peace, be still" to troubled souls. At least as often, that voice speaks, "Go and I'll be with you," to gifted Christ-followers open to God's next great adventure.

These are some of the themes congregations might celebrate to see more solution-oriented engagement in their communities:

- *They Are Attentive.* Vital parishes incubate kingdom attentiveness. Members in these faith communities are trained how to be alert to God's voice in their personal devotion. They also are encouraged to listen for opportunities to live out their faith in missional ways. When God prompts, the parish cheers. Rather than questioning the wisdom of taking holy risks, the healthy church invites every person to listen and follow as the Spirit leads. The result is an animated, expectant fellowship waiting for the next report of God's creativity in the life of one of their friends. Christianity ceases to be a spectator sport. There emerges a rhythm of waiting, listening, and then acting on what the Spirit says. While enacting, the congregation promotes reflective moments, rest stops along the journey, when we can sense what God is doing in us as well as what God is doing through us.

- *They Are Gifted.* Multiple times in Scripture we see God reminding people of their giftedness. To a Moses trying to beg off his next assignment by saying he had nothing to offer, God asks, "What is that in your hand?" To the overseers of the building of the place of worship, God names the craftsmen who would do the job with excellence. To the early church looking for resources to care for the burgeoning community, God raises up generous leaders ready to sell all they had.

- *They Are Called.* Each of us has particular assets useful for divine purposes. Our yes to God's voice is the starting point.

Unlike the standard contract where we sign only after reading the fine print, we grow to trust God's goodness to the point of signing a blank page first, one where the details are not yet clear, knowing nothing can occur without being filtered through God's mercy. Saying yes to the One who will always be with us gets easier over time. We learn that the One who calls us is faithful beyond our wildest imaginations.

- *They Are Authorized.* We also discover that callings are not just for the professional clergy. God has known us before we were born and has designed us with foresight. Every human being is created in God's image with purpose. For the willing, that purpose is lived out with the help of the Holy Spirit to do good in the lives of others. God shows up in schoolteachers and housekeepers, executives and contractors. Life as it is meant to be for us may entail multiple careers. It will always yield meaning and fruit as we live open to God's leading. Life lived 24-7-365 as a follower of Jesus means we have spiritual impact around the clock. We are changed and so are our coworkers as they experience Christ in us. Neighbors notice counter-cultural values in our witness. Our kindness and integrity in the supermarkets and restaurants point to Christ. Our diligence in being light and salt in every arena of our lives gives testimony in our relationships as we embrace God's calling in our lives.

- *They Are Cultivated.* The church provides the community in which we mature personally and discern corporately. Seldom does a calling come fully fleshed out in our minds. It often comes as an idea, maybe even a wild one that requires wise counsel to be fully apprehended. Our brothers and sisters listen with us, ask important questions, weigh merits on the scale of Scripture, and help propose initial experiments as we test our call. Many times calls are not only confirmed in a single person; they are confirmed in a small group of people to whom the Spirit has been speaking. The Lord is as capable of influencing teams of people as individuals.

- *They Are Sent.* Once a calling is discerned and initial forays into that calling are planned, seek partners. Where has God already set the stage for your calling? There may be people doing similar activities in your neighborhood. There may be funders looking for someone to implement a strategy that will meet a discrete need. There may be other congregations sensing the same call. Test the Spirit and know that there are likely others God has been speaking to as well. Callings are seldom ex nihilo; there are usually others called in the same general direction.

Why Some Ideas Never Live: Five Solution-Busters

Oliver Wendell Holmes once sought to fan the flames of human ingenuity with this cautionary observation: "Many people die with their music still in them. Why is this so? Too often it is because they are always getting ready to live. Before they know it, time runs out" (Holmes 1919). In other words, some of the world's best ideas have never seen the light of day. Having arisen brightly in the mind of a would-have-been world changer, that idea is doused out, usually because of the difficulties that go with starting anything. Like the law of inertia reminds us: getting a stationary, comfortable, or immobilized thing moving is the hardest part. There may be many reasons an idea dies an untimely death. In this chapter, we capture at least five obstacles that prevent ordinary people from making an extraordinary difference in the world around them. We want to describe these as solution-busting syndromes, and go beyond these to offer a single starting place for overcoming them. These solution-busters are:

- *The Passivity Problem—"If I Ignore It, It'll Go Away."* When faced with a complex problem it is natural to assume someone must already be at work on it. So, we deny or delay getting informed or involved. We wait. We worry. We walk away. And if the problem ceases to go away, or ceases to be merely theoretical by aggravating our personal comfort zones, then we will act (or react).

- *The Paralysis Problem—"It's Too Big for Me."* Sometimes large-scale social problems (often backed up by authoritative statistical reports that use terms like "two million affected," or, "we need four million dollars more to make a difference," or, "unchanged since 1974," or, "eight out of ten die every year unless you . . . ," or, "incurable case of . . . ," or, "save the children") can numb the average person into a case of absolute helplessness. The very scale and scope (often necessarily) used in the marketing by change advocates to raise the awareness of the problem can complicate the average person's ability to respond to the invitation to get involved in a way that feels equal to the challenge. And sometimes writing a "whatever you give will help" check just will not satisfy the conscience of someone who has seen that a big problem exists, but they can't imagine how their mere pittance will make a difference in light of the insurmountable odds that were used to describe the dilemma.

- *The Purse Problem—"My Pockets Aren't Deep Enough."* It's easy to see a social problem or hear an emotional appeal for money and feel like your meager offering amounts to very little when the plate gets passed through the pews. We think too easily that major donors have a major impact. We know some problems can be expensive. Things such as: environmental issues; medical and health care; nutrition deprivation; educational access and quality; international economic crises; graft and corruption; engineering-based development solutions; crime and incarceration; war and conflict-based problems; or political, ideological, and religious oppression result in the belief that only major infusions of cash will make a difference. And if we are a work-a-day person, with limited funds leftover at the end of the month, it's hard to imagine how our giving can effect lasting change. This scarcity view of what I have, you have, and they have limits the ability to see *all* the resources we may have available to us together in tackling social challenges.

- *The Permission Problem—"Only Professionals Need Apply."* Some people are professionals. These people have prepared themselves for career-level engagement, have been certified into a body of literature, practices, and ethical codes that separate their involvement from that of laypersons, volunteers and amateurs, those who are untrained and who lack expertise. This problem is especially true in churches and religiously based organizations that tend to be made up of believers who live with a kind of readiness to be used of God to change the world. When faced with an invitation to indeed change the world, such believers might find they are either required to get approval from pastors or official ministry managers, instead of just jumping in to offer what they can, as best they can. Some ministry leaders or their parent organizations, for all kinds of legitimate legal, ethical, and strategic reasons, may indeed require clearance or approval processes for non-clergy or non-staff.

- *The Plan Problem—"I'm Going to Ask for Help."* Some challenges can appear so daunting, so impenetrable, that the eyes of would-be volunteers and joiners glaze over, and there seems to be no way of getting started. As is true of most social problems, the causes are many and the solutions are seldom singular. These problems require multiple approaches. These problems require partial responses. These problems invite thoughtfully designed, long-term, phased-in strategies involving multiple types of resource support. These problems demand a plan, a process.

"Withness": The Partnering Reflex

When God chooses to change the world, he seems to do so by burdening a choice person. They see something that needs to be made right. They hear something that requires a response. They see how their skills, their background, their community can be of assistance to another person, another family, another community. This person who now carries a social burden, in turn is tasked with inviting others into a journey of shared hard work. Together, they achieve more than had the person acted alone. It's called the *partnering reflex*. And it changes the acts of one into the acts of the many.

This pattern of missional multiplication can be seen quite clearly in the book of Acts. In the eleventh chapter, the Gentiles of Antioch have begun to respond in growing numbers to the gospel invitation: "The Lord's power was with them, and a large number came to believe and turned to the Lord" (v. 21 CEB). This development, a genuine surprise for the Jewish leaders in Jerusalem, triggers an investigation. They dispatch a trusted worker, a man by the name of Barnabas.

As Barnabas arrives he is arrested by what he sees: (1) God is at work among this burgeoning community of new Gentile believers, and (2) if he is to be faithful to this clear movement of God, he had better mobilize some help. Then, one of the most important examples of strategic mission unfolds before the reader's eyes with so little fanfare that it is easily missed, *Barnabas leaves!* That's right: it's the largest religious revival in history, an opportunity for Barnabas to be crowned in history as the apostle to the Gentiles, and he bypasses his opportunity for fame and celebrity by trekking almost four hundred kilometers to go to the back roads of Damascus.

Why would anyone do such a thing? Has he left because of contribution-killing obstacles? Barnabas knows that if the new community is to survive, it needs resources. And in his mind, the primary resource needed on that scene was found in the person of an eccentric little rabbi whose reputation was quite questionable at the time. He went looking for Saul of Tarsus. In the person of Saul, who we would come to know eventually as Paul the apostle, Barnabas found resources sufficient to the strategy to which he had been called: "Barnabas went to Tarsus in search of Saul. When he found him, he brought him to Antioch. They were there for a whole year, meeting with the church and teaching large numbers of people" (Acts 11:25–26 CEB).

In the person of Paul, Barnabas found a partner. And the rest, as they say, is history. Or perhaps we might say, church history. Barnabas's selfless act of partnering made possible not only the survival of the new community of believers in Antioch, but the entire, worldwide Christian movement. He sought a resource, a person. And then, they organized what could probably be called a Bible and ministry school that lasted for an entire year. They innovated new solutions together that yielded results like nothing that had been seen in the history of God's people. And as the Scriptures note: "The disciples were called Christians first at Antioch" (Acts 11:26).

We believe God's method of transforming people, churches, and communities remains the same, one life multiplied for many. All of these contribution-killing obstacles described above share one thing in common: the obstacles maintain their hold over us as long as we tackle them alone. However, just by adding one other person, perhaps just a few others, everything changes in all of these areas.

By adding the capacity of just a few well-selected partners, real capacity for change gets accomplished. This is what we call the *partnership solution*. It's you plus others. Here is the principle:

The Partnering Reflex Principle: it is better to move slower by adding the power of a few partners who will strengthen the solution, than to rush forward alone with the questionable power of what only one person might achieve alone.

In other words, with one, you are alone. But with just a few others, you gain exponential capacity to transform the situation. But what is partnership? In his very useful book *Well Connected: Releasing the Power, Restoring the Hope Through Kingdom Partnerships*, Phil Butler offers this definition: "Any group of individuals or organizations, sharing a common interest, who regularly communicate, plan, and work together to achieve a common vision beyond the capacity of any one of the individual partners." He adds: "Partnerships don't exist just to share information or encourage fellowship. Information and encouragement are part of the partnership process. But they are means to an end, not the partnership's purpose" (Butler 2005). The combined efforts of the many almost always prevail over the best intentions of the solo heroic operator. Let's reconsider briefly the five obstacles outlined above, but this time with the added possibilities of capacity-building partnerships considered:

* *From Passivity to Engagement—"I Must Take a Step."* Every hard problem ever solved required a first step. Some solutions come only as people get inside of them to really see the problem up close. And what most solutionaries find is this: they were never alone. If it's a social problem, that means others in the community are affected by it, and they probably have not been waiting for others to rescue them, but just might welcome the contributions of willing friends who care about their plight.
* *From Paralysis to Conversation—"I'm Not the Only One Who Cares."* Most of the time when statistics are used to describe the scope of a challenge, these require a little more information on the ground to understand the true nature of the

problem. This is where seeking learning conversations with others who also care about the situation become important.

♦ *From Purse-Strapped to Partner-Backed—"I Have This to Offer."* As long as we are working alone on a big resistant problem, then it is easy to weigh our limited resources, and be found wanting. Here we ask, "What do *I* care about, and can *I* afford it?" But why would we do this when it is not possible that we are the lone person seeing or being impacted by the problem? Instead we must ask, "Who else cares about what I care about, and how can *we* afford it?" By acknowledging the natural partners already at work on the problem or opportunity, we join their momentum. Money is seldom the true hindrance in creating solutions; collaboration costs often are. It takes more time. It takes humility. It takes caring about others beside yourself who are helping in the work, not only those you aim to help.

♦ *From No Permission to Co-Mission—"My Authority Matters Too."* What is an expert except someone who has gone beyond his or her first exposure to a topic and continued learning? They were once new to the problem or opportunity too. Your curiosity, your conscience, your calling all matter just as does theirs. And in the case of ministry strategies, you have to decide on which side of the clergy/laity debate to stand. This debate involves competing views on who is allowed to offer ministry, for example, only those with ordination credentials and ministerial training or all equipped "saints for the work of ministry" (see Ephesians 4:10–16 NKJV). The debate usually resolves on the agreement that all believers are called to offer themselves in ministry to their worlds and share the same authority to do so, but that some are invited by organizations such as churches, denominations, and charities to do so as careers (and often are required to achieve education and credentials that certify they have done so). But seldom does anyone question whether the average person has a part to play, but rather to ask, "What is that part?"

♦ *From No Plan to Preparation—"I'm Going to Ask for Help."* Flying by the seat of our pants or making it up as we go seldom solves big problems. Humility demands that we learn from others, and that we approach these challenges in a thoughtful, well-considered manner. The preparation that precedes plans often makes the difference between solutions that are durable over those that cause more problems than they address. For planning, cause, calendar, capacity, costs, and criteria are the ones that ultimately make the most lasting difference.

The "Social" in Social Entrepreneurship: *The Collaboratory Approach*

Words matter. And the word "social" in front of "entrepreneurship," is a pretty important word, especially for those motivated by their Christian faith through their endeavors. This kind of entrepreneurship differs perhaps in motive, ends,

From Passive Observer . . .

From Obstacles

- From Passivity to Engagement—*I Must Take a Step.*
- From Paralysis to Conversation—*I'm Not the Only One Who Cares.*
- From Purse-Strapped to Partner-Backed—*I Have This to Offer.*
- From No Permission to Co-Mission—*My Authority Matters Too.*
- From No Plan to Preparation—*I'm Going to Ask for Help.*

To Opportunities

To Partnered Solutionary.

From Passive to Partnered Illustration
Figure One

and means from those usually associated with the for-profit-focused business launch. The difference is neither one of kind nor degree, but rather of *focus*. By "kind," this is what is meant: social entrepreneurship is like any other kind of business entrepreneurship. By "degree," it is meant: social entrepreneurship is not different from any other kind of business entrepreneurship. At its base, a social entrepreneurial venture must be good business. This will be important and discussed later on. By "degree" it is also meant: social entrepreneurship is neither better than, nor less than, any other entrepreneurial business endeavor. Social entrepreneurship is on a continuum of business service offerings. However, by "focus" it is meant: social entrepreneurship derives its distinct place in business practice by virtue of its motivation, its involvement of others, and its social impact. And this difference makes all the difference in the world between entrepreneurial business launches and social entrepreneurial business launches.

People are one of the key resources in the social entrepreneur's toolkit. In contrast to some of the key elements of a for-profit business launch, which often begins with goods, services, or experiences offered to add value, the social entrepreneur must offer these and then some. However, they must do so with a specific social-impact vision in mind. The for-profit business venture may accept as its mission to be the "return of profits to the shareholder," but the social entrepreneur cannot afford to take care of shareholder profits only; they must reckon with a wider definition of that which can be considered profit. While the bottom line is important for the traditional business entrepreneur, the social entrepreneur must emphasize that bottom line of healthy profit plus the bottom line of adding value to society.

For the social entrepreneur, the following might suggest a working list of the usual partnership suspects: cause, counsel, capital, and connection. This is the Collaboratory Map. The

Collaboratory Map offers a picture of the multiple partners available to the entrepreneur. *Note: a worksheet is provided later in this chapter.*

◆ *The Cause Dimension.* The first dimension describes partners who fuel the *cause.* The cause dimension is the reason the new organization is coming into existence. The cause describes *what you care about, who you care about,* and *who cares about you* (and your success as an organization). Some of these partners include: community members and users; recipients of programming; operational staff such as chief executive, staff members, and volunteer team; activist ethicists and other thought leaders.

◆ *The Counsel Dimension.* The counsel dimension of collaboration celebrates that many potential partners exist who not only share the cause, but might contribute specific experience,

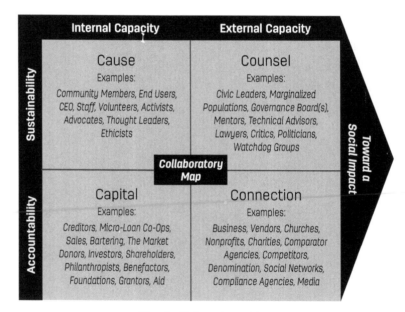

The Collaboratory Map
Figure Two

skills, and credibility to the project by offering their support, wisdom, and technical expertise. Some of the examples of this dimension include: civic leaders, members of marginalized populations, various forms of government support, consultants, mentors and technical advisors such as lawyers, CPAs, financial advisors, politicians, and watchdog groups.

♦ *The Capital Dimension.* The capital dimension focuses on those partners and resources that can be leveraged to accelerate, deepen, and extend solutions. Examples of partnership in the capital dimension include: creditors, micro-loan co-ops, salespersons, the market and its forces, donors, shareholders, philanthropists, foundations, and grantors.

♦ *The Connection Dimension.* The connection dimension represents all of those relationships external to your organization that would complement, extend, and strengthen the achievement of your mission. Examples of connections include: other businesses, vendors, nonprofits, charities, churches, synagogues and temples, comparator agencies, competitors, parent organizations such as denominations or nongovernmental organizations, compliance agencies, and the various media and their outlets.

Along the left-hand side of the Collaboratory Map, two words appear: "Sustainability," and "Accountability." These two themes are basic for the success of any lasting start-up venture. Few social problems are of such scale that they can be eradicated by the temporary efforts of amateurs who intend to attend to the matter as part-time dabblers. Usually, social problems equal to the call of the social entrepreneur are complex, multicausal, widespread, and expensive to transform. Without a sustainability focus that aims for persistent, educated, and resource-plying efforts until indicators of change begin to yield to the dedication of the social entrepreneurs and their collaborators, transformation will be short-lived and disappointing.

Short-term efforts often create more problems than they ultimately address. Sustainability functions like an objective, a goal, a strategy horizon. However, sustainability as a goal must be met with criteria and processes that keep the pressure exerted and keep the cause fueled with good thinking and goodwill. Accountability offers the checks and balances to ensure that while social entrepreneurs mean to do good, they do well at the same time. Accountability supplies the report card; sustainability provides the finish line to know when the course is nearly over.

In addition to these two value and measurement dimensions on the Collaboratory Map, the direction of focus also provides guidance to the partnering efforts. The cause dimension and capital dimension tend to deepen the internal capacity of the organization to advance the mission. These partners appear to focus inward on the organization's internal needs, so that these may be leveraged for external service. The external counsel and connection dimension infuse the organization and its operations, resource use, and measurement with wisdom, synergy, and a context for widespread influence. These elements make up the drivers of the Collaboratory Map.

The Collaboratory Worksheet: *Clean Water for All Project*

Current Buy-In = ✗   Desired Buy-In = ✔

Aim	Stakeholders Types	Stakeholder Name	Not Involved	Obtain Advice	Obtain Assist	Obtain Authority	Action Required
Accountability — **Cause**	Community Members, End Users, Customers, Consumers, Recipients	Women Water Carriers, Sara	✗ ——→		✔		*Invite Sara, CEO WWC*
	CEO/Exec. Director, Operational Team(s), Volunteers	Ollie Jones, Finance Mgr			✗ ——→	✔	*Send New Budget*
	Moral Support, Activists, Advocates, Thought Leaders, Ethicists	Alice J., Well Watered, Blog			✗ ——→	✔	*Send Press Release*
	Change Agents, Entrepreneurs, Communities of Practice	Charity Water, Liaison Office	✗	✔			*Go On, Make that Call!*
Counsel	Local Leaders, Civic Councils, Marginalized Voices, Incubators	• Mayor's Ofc • Chamber, Dir.			✗ —→ ✔	✗	*Provide 4th Qtr Report*
	Advisory, Policy, Governance Board(s), Trustees/Owners	Policy Board Chair, Cindy				✗ —→ ✔	*Get Travel Policy Done*
	Consultants, Coaches						

Collaboratory Map, Illustrated

Figure Three

The Collaboratory Map allows a social entrepreneurial team to identify their own community of concern for the social issue that matters to them most. It allows teams to not only know they are not alone, but also not to go it alone, by developing a collaborative circle of others who care about similar issues you care about and everyone who cares about your success.

Essentially, the Collaboratory Map rises and falls on your readiness to recruit the help you need to your cause. While not everything need be in place to gain the attention of potential stakeholders, volunteers, or staff, you must be clear about a few basic principles of recruitment to get the help you need. Consider these "readiness to recruit" suggestions:

◆ Be ready to unapologetically tell potential stakeholders about the state of the problem as you currently see it, and why you are invested personally in solving or seizing upon it.

◆ Be ready to describe to potential stakeholders why you think they might be or have a missing piece of the puzzle that would make a difference in the opportunity before you. If you have a square hole, and the person is a square peg, they will understand why you have come to them!

◆ Be ready to be specific when making "The Ask." If you need them to coach your board of directors for four hours, twice a month for the next six months, make the invitation exactly that specific. Avoid general invitations that are open to various interpretations such as, "Hey, can you help out my new board?" Such a vague invitation may provoke fear that you want all of their spare time, or that you want them to join the board as its chair or many other impractical ideas that allows them to conclude that they are a round peg for your square hole.

◆ Be ready to do some preparation before you ask potential partners to join your venture. A stakeholder may be a volunteer or may be a paid professional who is sought to assist the implementation of your idea or project. But the best recruitment conversations follow the kind of advice given in Helen Little's *Volunteers: How to Get Them, How to Keep Them* (1999): a manageable task, one matching interests with capacity, an answer to the "why question," written instructions, a reasonable deadline, freedom to complete in their own time and without interruption, training, resources, feedback, and of course, appreciation and compensation (as required or needed).

The Collaboratory Map offers the social entrepreneur a planning device to think through what each type of potential partner might need from you in order to make their best contribution to your idea, project, or organization. Good collaboration, good partnerships, require thoughtful planning.

Conclusion: Congregations that Celebrate and Send

He was one of those hardened personalities with off-color stories to match. He doubted the church would let him in the door, but his wife insisted they go to the Christmas Eve service. People with his reputation did not go to church. Imagine his surprise when he discovered one or two acquaintances in the same service. If they were welcome in the church, maybe he could hazard coming back a second time.

One of the opportunities to serve that he noticed early on was an appeal for pickup trucks for delivering used appliances to families. Volunteers would pick up used stoves or refrigerators from donors and haul them to homes needing them. He started offering his truck and help once a month. Over time, that involvement grew to repairing appliances as well as delivering them. His skill at appliance repair and his ability to find homes needing the help resulted in the eventual creation of a 501(c)3 corporation, complete with a twelve-foot covered trailer and rented warehouse space. The volunteer staff grew to support deliveries three times a week.

Somewhere, when he was serving monthly, he began to grasp God's promise for himself. His own spirit began to believe that God could change him as well. He made a commitment to follow Jesus. The congregation discipled him in personal devotion and called out God's best in him through the corporate disciplines of worship, fellowship, and obedience to God's voice.

When the church held its first celebration of volunteers, he was one of the honorees. Each recipient was introduced in a "this is your life" format. As the presenter began to describe his faithful outreach, with each sentence it became clear they were talking about him. People began to smile; he began to weep. "I don't deserve this. I'm just trying to follow God's voice. I'm no one special."

That is normal for healthy congregations. Common obedience to God's leading yields beautiful transformation. They cultivate the solutionaries in their midst. They know that the "priesthood of believers" does not get worked out only in volunteer positions or service teams on Sundays. Some of these members express their ministries in ordinary ways, on ordinary days, in ordinary places, but do so with extraordinary results when they partner with the gifts within, the congregation beside, and touch the communities beyond the four walls of the church.

Using the Collaboratory Map (Worksheet)

* Step One. In column one, planners review examples of stake-holder types available in most communities.

* Step Two. This review helps the planner generate a list of actual stakeholder names (column two). Contact information for these stakeholders could also be gathered and added here.

* Step Three. The next four columns represent specific commit-ments that planners seek from the stakeholders, as well as their level of "Current Buy-In" (represented by "X"). The aim here is to place a "✓" for the "Desired Buy-In." The choices include: "Not Involved" (Yet); "Obtain Advice;" "Obtain Assistance," or technical help; and "Obtain Authority," or permission. Specific actions required of the stakeholder are described in the last column.

* Step Four. Plot the stakeholder's degree of "Current Buy-In" with an "X" and also a "✓" for the "Desired Buy-In." Then, in the last column, name actions required of each stakeholder (not you), in order to be moved from "Current Buy-In" to "Desired Buy-In" level.

* Step Five. Initiate recruitment conversations, inviting the stakeholder to join your idea, project, or organization in the specific area of contribution you have identified.

The Collaboratory Worksheet
Current Buy-In = ✗   Desired Buy-In = ✔

Aim		Stakeholders Types	Stakeholder Name	Not Involved	Obtain Advice	Obtain Authority	Obtain Assist	Action Required
Accountability	Cause	Community Members, End Users, Customers, Consumers, Recipients						
		CEO/Exec. Director, Operational Team(s), Volunteers						
		Moral Support, Activists, Advocates, Thought Leaders, Ethicists						
		Change Agents, Entrepreneurs, Communities of Practice						
	Counsel	Local Leaders, Civic Councils, Marginalized Voices, Incubators						
		Advisory, Policy, Governance Board(s), Trustees/Owners						
		Consultants, Coaches, Mentors, Technical Advisors, Lawyers, CPA						
		Critics, Opponents, Competitors, Politicians, Mediators, Watchdogs						

Sustainability	*Capital*	Creditors, Stewards, Heritage Investors, Microenterprise Cooperatives					
		Sales, Bartering, Market Forces, ROI, Brokers, Stock Market					
		Funders, Donors, Investors, Venture Capitalists, Shareholders					
		Philanthropists, Benefactors, Foundations, Grantors, Aid					
	Connection	Businesses, Industry Segments, Vendors, Government Providers					
		Social Sector Providers, Churches, Non-Profits, Charities, Economic/ Community Development					
		Complementing, Comparator & Competitor Groups, Guilds					
		Parent Org., Incubators, Networks, Compliance Agencies, Media					

Discussion Questions

---

1. Consider the list of characteristics outlined in the chapter: congregations are *attentive, gifted, called, authorized, cultivated,* and *sent.* What ingredients are present in your congregation that encourage social entrepreneurship ventures? What ingredients are missing?

2. Five "Solution-Busters" are listed in the chapter, described as a shift from *Passive to Partnered.* Have you ever experienced these obstacles? Can you list others?

3. Partnership is not always the easiest route when one is trying to get things done—it takes more time, people, and resources. But, that is also a reason for cultivating partnering as a reflex. Coordinating more time, people, and resources may be just what some ideas and programs need. Can you think of circumstances in which partnering is an ideal solution, and when it may not be the best solution? What are the drawbacks in either case?

4. A Collaboratory Map is offered to illustrate that a community of stakeholders is almost always present when a new socially entrepreneurial idea, project, or organization is coming into being. The Collaboratory Map implies you have to recruit people to join your idea, project, or organization. Consider the "readiness to recruit" suggestions in the chapter. Which of these steps come easily for you and your project? Which ones require more preparation before you invite stakeholders? Could a mentor or coach be useful to you, even before you begin to approach other stakeholders?

5. The Collaboratory Map emphasizes a community of stakeholders in the areas of *cause, counsel, capital,* and *connection.* Which of these areas become immediately important to the ideas that you and your project may require? What steps do you need to take in order to get stakeholders on your team?

Works Cited

Bitzer, Lloyd. 1968. "The Rhetorical Situation." *Philosophy and Rhetoric* 1:1–14.

Butler, Phil. 2005. *Well Connected: Releasing the Power, Restoring the Hope Through Kingdom Partnerships.* Federal Way, WA: Authentic Books.

Crouch, Andy. 2012. "What's So Great About 'The Common Good'? Why Christians Need to Revive the Historically Rich Phrase." *Christianity Today.* October 12, 2012. http://www.christianitytoday. com/ct/2012/november/whats-so-great-about-common-good .html.

Holmes, Oliver Wendell, Sr. 1919. "The Voiceless." *Bartlett's Familiar Quotations,* 10th edition. New York: Little, Brown and Company Publishing.

Little, Helen. 1999. *Volunteers: How to Get Them, How to Keep Them.* Naperville, IL: Panacea Press.

Wheatley, Margaret. 1999. *Leadership and the New Science: Discovering Order in a Chaotic World.* San Francisco, CA: Berrett-Koehler.

Note

2. In his seminal article, "The Meaning of Social Entrepreneurship" (2015), the late professor Greg Dees tapped into a description of business practice that captured the imagination of change agents who both respected the traditional bottom line of business, but who cared also about the multiple bottom lines of social impact. He described social entrepreneurs as change agents whose mission is social value, instead of private; who pursue opportunities advancing that mission; engage in continuous refinement; risk limited resources; and exhibit high accountability for outcomes to a wide array of stakeholders (not only shareholders, as would be expected in traditional business models).

Additional Recommended Resources

Article

Dees, Gregory. 2015. "The Meaning of Social Entrepreneurship."
Stanford University. Social Entrepreneurship Resources Hub.
http://sehub.stanford.edu.

Books

Bornstein, David. 2007. *How to Change the World*. New York: Oxford
University Press.

Collier, Paul. 2008. *The Bottom Billion*. New York: Oxford University Press.

Elkington, John, and Hartigan, Pamela. 2008. *The Power of
Unreasonable People: How Social Entrepreneurs Create Markets That
Change the World*. Boston, MA: Harvard Business Review Press.

Foster, William Landes, Peter Kim, and Barbara Christiansen. 2009.
"Ten Nonprofit Funding Models." *Stanford Social Innovation Review*.
Vol. 47 (Spring): 32–39.

Nicholls, Alex, ed. 2008. *Social Entrepreneurship: New Models of
Sustainable Social Change*. New York: Oxford University Press.

Novogratz, Jacqueline. 2009. *The Blue Sweater: Bridging the Gap between
Rich and Poor in an Interconnected World*. New York: Rodale Books.

Perrini, Francesco, ed. 2006. *The New Social Entrepreneurship: What
Awaits Social Entrepreneurial Ventures?* Northampton, MA: Edward
Elgar Publishing.

Prahalad, C. K. 2005. *The Fortune at the Bottom of the Pyramid*. Upper
Saddle River, NJ: Pearson Education, Inc.

Zeigler, Rafael, ed. 2009. *An Introduction to Social Entrepreneurship:
Voices, Preconditions, Contexts*. Northampton, MA: Edward Elgar
Publications.

Media

The New Heroes (PBS Series). Excerpt from website: "A four-hour
video series, hosted by Robert Redford, which tells the dramatic
stories of twelve social entrepreneurs who bring innovative,
empowering solutions to the most intractable social problems
around the world. Each story in this unique series illustrates the
amazing changes that are possible when an innovative idea is

coupled with optimism, a strategy for action, and a passionate
belief in human potential." www.pbs.org/opb/thenewheroes.

Heroes from a Small Planet (Frontline Series). Excerpt from website:
"Our 'Heroes' series highlights the work of social entrepreneurs
who are providing systemic and sustainable business solutions to
improve the lives of millions of people in the developing world."
http://www.pbs.org/frontlineworld/stories/socialentrepreneurs
.html.

Top 11 TED Talks on Social Entrepreneurship. Excerpt from website:
"TED talks are inspiring, often spurring people to action, who
are looking to change the world. While there are many top 10
or top 20 lists of most inspiring TED talks ever, there aren't
many that single out individuals who have had enduring social
impact through their work. We took our time to scour through
many TED talks and handpick these 11 videos that highlight
social entrepreneurs, academics and practitioners who have had
a profound impact in the world of social entrepreneurship."
http://social.yourstory.com/2013/08/inspiring-ted-talks-power
-of-social-entrepreneurship.

Top 10 Social Entrepreneurs of All Time. Excerpt from website: "While
it is admirable to build a successful business of any kind, some
entrepreneurs do more than just make a profit with the fruits of
their labor. Some actually help others, bringing resources, opportunities, training, and other assets to those who need them most.
These social entrepreneurs use their know-how and business
savvy to make the world a better place, combining a traditional
business model with a pressing social mission in ways that have
been helping to make big changes in places around the world
for decades. Here, we highlight just a few of the standout social
entrepreneurs who're showing that successful businesses don't
have to just watch the bottom line and can truly be socially
and environmentally conscious." http://www.onlinecollege
.org/2012/06/26/the-10-greatest-social-entrepreneurs-all-time/.

Five Inspiring Videos of Social Entrepreneurs. Excerpt from website:
"A list of five inspirational videos featuring successful social
entrepreneurs. The following is a list of five inspirational videos
featuring successful social entrepreneurs to give us some encouragement and to remind us that we may be lonely, but we are not
alone." http://www.socialenterprisebuzz.com/2012/11
/01/5-inspiring-youtube-videos-of-social-entrepreneurs/.

CHAPTER SEVEN

EXPLORATION PRAYER TRILOGY

Dwight Gibson

As you embark on your own journey into the possibility of being a social entrepreneur, look on this as a journey of exploration: exploring yourself, your own ideas, communities in need, and especially how God might want to be using you to change the world. Every journey has a beginning, middle, and an end, and such a journey of exploration is no exception. We offer these prayers as a way to begin your own exploration on this journey on a daily basis.

Morning Exploration Prayer

Lord, today is a new day.

With expectation and excitement,
    I explore with anticipation.

May Your thoughts guide the pondering that
    will open new insight and potential
    in a world of puzzling problems and
    exponential possibilities.

In looking for landmarks may I seek truth,
    goodness, and beauty, focusing on those
    areas that bring You honor and
    illuminate the intricacies of Your
    creative hand in the universe.

In seeking the way forward, guide my steps to
    honor You, aligned with Your plan for
    flourishing in all creation.

When discoveries are made, may all rejoice
    in a job well done and may what is found
    be for Your glory and the good
    of all creation, both for today and
    in the years to come.

At the end of the journey, help me to have found
    wisdom and use it as a foundation
    for explorations yet to be,

Amen.

Exploration Midday Prayer

Today is known. My eyes see its hours.
Tomorrow is unknown.
Its potential anticipated.

To see beyond what is known, I must
imagine, wonder, and explore.
What is beyond is unknown,
awaiting discovery.

Lord, help me to use my gifts to explore.
Let me understand the truths You
ordained, Your great design in
yesterday, today, and forever.

Your words are a light unto my path.
The universe awaits discovery.
Your plan is the truth of the ages for
the flourishing of life, in worlds known
and yet to be known.

I am an explorer for the glory of God.
Seeing beyond, this gift is not
for me alone.

May it benefit the whole of humanity,
revealing Your creation to all,

Amen.

Evening Exploration Praise

From the rising of the sun to the going down
    of the same, Your name is to be praised,
    O Lord.

You have brought light from darkness,
    known from unknown,
    discovery from chaos.

The flag has been planted.
    The bell has been rung.
    The victory has been won.

Returning home, we are changed.
    We praise You for wisdom found,
    for destination reached,
    for journey completed.

From the rising of the sun to
    the going down of the same,
    Your name is to be praised, O Lord,

Amen.